GOLDEN
UNIVERSE

TANGO

50 KEYS

Cambalache

Tango. 1934.

That the world has been and will
always be filth,
I always knew,
In five hundred and six and in year
2000 too.
There have always been thieves,
Machiavels and deceived,
Contented and gloomy people,
Values and fakes.
But, that the twentieth century
is a display of insolent wickedness
there's no one who can deny it.
We live wallowing in this muddle,
all in the same sticky mud,
everyone being messed up.

Turns out it's quite the same today
to be righteous or a traitor,
ignorant, learned, or thief,
generous or swindler.
Everything is the same
Nothing is better,
It doesn't matter being just an ass
or a renowned professor .
There are no more flunking
nor promotions.
The cheaters
have caught up with us.
If one man lives like an imposter
and another steals his way to the top
It makes no difference if he is a priest
a mattress-maker, king of clubs
a sassy or a cop.

What a lack of respect!
What a way to run over reason.
Anybody is a Gentleman,
anybody is a thief.
Arm in Arm with Stavisky goes
Don Bosco and La Mignon
Don Chicho and Bonaparte
Carnera and San Martín...
Much like in the junk-shop windows
life appears as we live it,
all mixed up,
wounded by some sword without rivets,
You see a Bible weeping
next to a water-heater...

Twentieth century!
problematic and feverish!
If you don't cry you don't get fed
and if you don't steal you're a dolt.
Go ahead! Keep it up!
that we're gonna reunite in the
furnace down below
Don't think anymore,
sit back,
you might have been born honest
but nobody gives a damn.
It's the same for one who works,
day and night like an ox,
one who lives from the others,
one who kills or heals
or one who lives outside the law.

Music & lyrics by:
Enrique Santos Discépolo

TANGO
50 KEYS
LAURA FALCOFF

GOLDEN COMPANY

© 2011 Golden Company SRL
Corrientes Ave. 989, Buenos Aires, Argentina.
www.goldencompany.com.ar

Book collection: Golden Universe.
Editors: Mr. Manuel Della Picca - Arch. Liliana I. Della Picca.
Author: Laura Falcoff.
Editorial Coordination: Lic. Pamela Della Picca.
General Coordination Assistant: Lic. Irina Guinovart.
Layout: Daniel Avinceta.
Cover Photo: Diana Martínez Lláser.
Translation: Sol Lorenzo.
Printed in China.

ACKNOWLEDGEMENT:
This book would have never been possible without the generous collaboration of the Photograph Department of the Archivo General de la Nación; Academia Nacional del Tango and his founder and president Horacio Ferrer; Casa Carlos Gardel Museum; Homero Manzione; Agustín Beltrame; Mimí Pinzón and Madreselva (cover photo and page 18); Irina Guinovart (page 49); Marseilles des Anges (page 49); Typical orchestra El Afronte (page 54); Antigüedades Shuk Hapispishin (page 63); Metrogas, Alejandro Lastiesas (page 63); Marcelo Bernadaz and Verónica Gardella (page 75); Eduardo Dosisto (page 77); Armesto Almacén Porteño (pages 93 and 95); Mansión Dandi Royal (pages 96, 139 and 166); Sister Solnicki (pages 96 and 139); Dimitri Fofana (page 129); Manu Lizarralde (page 139); Di Poggio (page 139); Gian Piero Cammarata (page 142); David López (page 143); Giannicola Lanzafame (page 145); Bajofondo Tango Club (page 152 and 153); Esquina Carlos Gardel (page 154, 155, 156 and 157); Bar Sur (page 66, 158 & 159); El Viejo Almacén (page 160); Madero Tango (page 161); Rivarola Family (page 166).

Falcoff, Laura
    Tango fifty keys. - 1a ed. - Buenos Aires : Golden Company, 2011.
    192 p. : il. ; 20x14 cm.

    Traducido por: María Sol Lorenzo
    ISBN 978-987-1820-00-9

    1. Tango. I. Lorenzo, María Sol, trad. II. Título.
    CDD 793.33

CONTENTS

Prologue

It is pertinent to ask why gathering fifty tango keys in a book, why not twelve, or twenty eight or thirty four. In the first place, we could say that one is at ease with round numbers and, for some reason, they straighten our thoughts. Moreover, no fewer than half a hundred topics could cover such a vast and complex phenomenon as tango is, even in a book on popularization of the tango, as this one intends to be.

The first steps of this work consisted purely of an accumulative process, which aimed at reaching the number fifty. Several items commenced to appear, some were considered and many others were discarded.

It would not be, as previously arranged with the publishers, a historical work, though some history sneaks through its pages. Biographies would not be included, except for the necessary ones, nor would it be predominantly anecdotal.

The result ended up being a combination of a panoramic approach with minimal details: from the milonga and the cafés of Buenos Aires to the kiss, horse racing, and the topic of the mother in tango lyrics. I would like to add that I made a special effort to make this book appeal to tango experts and novice alike. I hope I have succeeded.

Finally, I wish to thank Dana Frúgoli, Pablo Villarraza, Héctor Angel Benedetti and Héctor Larrea for their kind cooperation; also Irene Amuchástegui, for her cheerful and delightful friendship who also showed me the way through tango. And last but not least, to Mariano Etkin for his appreciated musical contribution and for listening to me with patience and consideration.

Laura Falcoff

Carlos Gardel

1

"He sings better every day", it is said of Carlos Gardel and, although seventy years have passed since his death, such expression is still in vogue. However, this incongruous saying embraces an irrefutable truth: Gardel sings better every day. In the first place, because to date no tango singer has eclipsed the tango star that Carlos Gardel was and is. Likewise, because his expression and voice will never be old-fashioned: When heard, Gardel always seems fresh and new, because, among other things, he is a singer that does not make a style out of emphasis and also because his extraordinary communicability does not fall into overacting. Finally, his perfect tuning, his exquisite taste and the way he puts music into words produces something unique in each song of his extensive repertoire.

If contemporary myths exist, then Carlos Gardel is a real one, partly built by himself based on everything he never said or on what he did say, but giving different versions in different moments. There are circumstances of Gardel's life that have remained a mystery, from his origins to love affairs. His actual date of birth, and particularly, his place of birth were an eternal controversy and although it appears to be definitely proved now that he was born in Toulouse, France, in 1890 and baptized under the name Charles Romuald Gardes, many Uruguayan voices continue to claim that he was born in Tacuarembó. Due to his early death in a tragic airplane crash in Medellín, Colombia, Gardel became a legend. Different versions spread, some affirmed that he did not die, others, that he did not appear in public because he was left disfigured.

Gardel was an exceptionally gifted artist who made his way in the world with minimum resources. His mother, who did the washing and ironing for others, was not in a position to give him money or afford his education, and the regular customers of the bars and cafés near the Abasto neighborhood, where he grew up and was nicknamed, "little French boy", were the first to hear his performances as singer.

Gardel produces his first tango recording in 1917, up to that moment his repertory fea-

From left to right:
Uruguayan musician
Luis Eduardo Casaravilla
Sienra, amateur singer
Ricardo Bonapelch,
Carlos Gardel and an
unidentified person
(Montevideo, no date)

13

tured mainly folk songs, and the song titled **Mi noche triste** (My sad night) by Pascual Contursi will be the first tango-song. Carlos Gardel evolved extraordinarily all through his career; he searched constantly for new possibilities, not only regarding the musical groups but also in his repertoire. Gardel was the composer and interpreter of his own songs, to mention some, the very well known **Mi Buenos Aires querido** (My beloved Buenos Aires), **Lejana tierra mía** (Far away home land), **Sus ojos se cerraron** (Her eyes closed shut), **El día que me quieras** (The day you love me), **Rubias de Nueva York** (Blondes from New York), all these written by lyricist Alfredo Le Pera.

Considering his international career, which includes films, no other Argentine singer managed, before or after, to equal Gardel. The Odeon label, about to close its Buenos Aires subsidiary after the 1929 crisis, was able to re-emerge thanks to a series of records previously recorded with Gardel and that were launched for sale with no hope.

First hundreds, and immediately after, thousands of requests were made to the record company that avoided bankruptcy.

Carlos Gardel's last recording was an advertisement for the Víctor label and for Paramount, which distributed his films.

At that time he had announced his next tour around Latin America and promised, among other things, more perfect recordings. He died three months later, on June 24, 1935.

Gardel with Mona Maris
in Film Cuesta Abajo
(Paramount, 1934)

2
Tango clothes

The typical outfit for a male tango dancer is a light white cloth scarf known as "lengue", a hat tilted to one side of the face, striped trousers held by suspenders and shiny pointy shoes. Let's get this straight: we refer to a dancer of a classic tango show. Along its side, women's clothes for tango shows in general consist of a short skirt with a deep slit on the side, a neckerchief tied in a knot tilted to one side, fishnet stockings and very high-heel shoes.

We will no longer see this type of outfit in a ballroom. The most conservative milonga habitué dancers usually dress in suit, tie and lace shoes, especially those who attend evening milongas; day and afternoon milongas display a more casual dressing. (Milongas: social tango dance events)

Women resort to more heterogeneous clothing, however, being pretty and young does not guarantee a successful time at a milonga, nor does wearing stunning clothes.

However, clothes are carefully selected and elegance is present in a variety of forms. It is quite common to find a lady coming from the street wearing her office outfit, going straight to the restrooms and in a few minutes is dress up in the most sumptuous and spectacular dress of her wardrobe. Lita Filippini, a dressmaker, is a frequent dancer of Sunderland Club in Villa Urquiza neighborhood and continues attending the dance floors as she did back in the 50's. Some years ago she as-

17

sured: "during my whole life, on each Saturday of milonga, I used a different dress and shoes; I have shoes to last a lifetime".

One of the most important pieces in a tango dancer outfit is, no doubt, the pair of shoes. Shoes must slide on the dance floor, hence rubber sole is not recommended and, although the shoes have to have good support, a rigid shoe is not suitable.

High heels are fundamental in the woman's outfit: as she moves backwards while dancing along the dance floor, flat shoes will not permit such movement or she will have to dance on tip toes. The worldwide diffusion of Tango brought enormous progress to the shoe design field, both for men and, above all, for women. Unimaginable colors, with stones and flowers, sumptuous glitter, imitation leather, furs, extreme high heels: a hilarious fantasy spreads on the dance floor and the sensuality of the feminine tango shoe can beat the most plunging neckline.

3
The milonga dancer

If in the old days the word "milonguero" was a sort of insult, now it is almost a title of nobility. The word "milonguero" refers to the tango dancer who frequented neighborhood clubs during the 40's and 50's. In those times, they were considered men of not-so-good reputation, layabouts, who practiced steps during the afternoons, and at nights used to frequent the ballrooms. But as time went by, tango music reappeared and expanded worldwide, and the surviving milongueros -inevitably men of middle-age or more- started to enjoy prestige and respect. They are not museum pieces, certainly not: the authentic milonguero, or at least the so-called milonguero, is today a highly requested coach, a coveted dancing partner, considered a fountain of wisdom and a reservoir of secrets and stories. In this new era, a great number of tango dancers paved their way by teaching, not only in Buenos Aires but also in the United States or Europe; some of them reached the stages while many others kept faithful to the simple pleasure of dancing.

The milonguero is capable of creating his personal style. No matter how many steps or how many figures he masters, he cannot lack elegance, musicality and, above all, must know how to "walk" the dance, which, according to many opinions, is the highest value and the most difficult task to achieve. Of course, there are young milongueros, young boys who take the tango to heart, who devote many hours to learning every day and uncountable night hours to dancing. It is not strange to see these youngsters jump from the dance-floor to the concert stage... being this their ambition.

Let's mention some milonguero dancers throughout different generations: *Tete:* retired municipal employee and dancer without equal, he would seldom skip a milonga night; *Puppy* and *Negro* Portalea, both passed away in year 2007, although having different styles, they shared a fine musicality, as well as *Petróleo, Finito, Pepito* Avellaneda*, Lampazo, el Negro Lavandina, el Chino Perico, el Flaco* Danny, Miguel Zotto; the latter being a successful international stage dancer who learned to dance in the milongas, by watching, practicing and following the example of wonderful intuitive artists.

4

The neighborhood

Buenos Aires neighborhoods are not one hundred, as evoked with enthusiasm by singer Alberto Castillo in a well-known waltz; in fact the municipal maps currently distinguish only forty eight districts. However, the tango has honored widely and with deep emotion each and every neighborhood in Buenos Aires; hence, the exaggerated counting may well be excused.

The simple definition in the dictionary states that neighborhood is each unit in which the city is divided. However, for the tango, neighborhood is much more than that: it is a live entity, boasting a smell of geranium and honeysuckle that will be missed forever once you leave it.

"Almagro, Almagro of my life, you were the soul of my dreams... How many nights of moon and faith, under your protection I knew to love…"

"I feel sorry of you Barrio de Flores, place of my childhood games, worn memories, love novel that evokes a romance of never ending joy."

"Boedo, your soul is full of emotions, the same as mine, as an open heart that is tired of waiting."

A rather exceptional example is the tango song about the so-called area Bajo Belgrano, a neighborhood that in past years was dedicated to horse racing activities and the nearby Palermo Hippodrome, and said tango is written in an optimistic present

time: "Bajo Belgrano, how healthy is your young breeze, bringing whistles, songs and laughter from the stud patios".

The typical neighborhood with low houses, where everybody knows each other, differs significantly from the city center, a place with night, trifling and dangerous life. The tango **No salgas de tu barrio** (Do not leave your neighborhood) warns: "Don't leave your mother, your street, your convent, or the ordinary boy who begged for your love".

In the tango **Muñeca brava** (Mad doll) the woman that chose to live a dissipate life cannot hide her origin to the man that met her when she was a little girl: "You, madam that speak French and lavishly throw money away, that dine with champagne, very *frappé*, and in the tango interweave your illusion… you are a biscuit of very arching eyelashes, Mad Doll, well valued! You are from the Trianón…from the Trianón of Villa Crespo. You, vamp… an occasion toy!".

One of the most beautiful titles of the tango repertory is called precisely **Barrio de tango** (Neighborhood of tango) and is dedicated to the Pompeya neighborhood: "A piece of neighborhood in Pompeya sleeping on the slopes of the embankment a streetlamp swinging in the barrier and a farewell mystery that the train sows neighborhood of tango, moon and mystery fareway streets, how are you now? Old friends I can no longer remember what have they done where could they be?".

5
The Milonga

Milonga, in addition to the same-name rhythm, is the public place where people get together to dance tango. However, if it comes to describing today's milonga, that definition is not enough. The big dance halls of old tango clubs, with its scheduled days for dance and dancers grouped by neighborhood and social class have virtually disappeared. In its place, the modern aficionado has a lot of alternatives to choose from, every time, every day, and all imaginable kinds of people. Let's see: a perpetual social and sport club of Villa Urquiza neighborhood is the headquarters of the best Buenos Aires milonga, the most traditional and respected for the quality of the tango that can be watched there. The club's basketball court, arranged with tables and chairs, where the dance takes place, lacks any sophistication and stands out against the evening elegance of ladies and gentlemen. This milonga's fame has travelled around the world and it is not unusual to find renown Argentine and foreign artists and intellectuals there, who cross the city on Saturday night simply to watch the experimented milongueros dancers. Many young people also attend that milonga to drink from the fountain of the best tango. On the other end, on Sunday nights, the bower of a park at Belgrano neighborhood shelters a completely informal milonga: there is no place to sit down, and coats, bags and shoes pile up at a corner; there is no entrance ticket, just a voluntary contribution and the range of ages and dance experience is exceptionally wide. The neighbors and the children that play at the park are usually the attentive spectators of the milonga. Between this milonga and the oldest gay milonga that is located at the financial district of Buenos Aires, there is a considerable distance. In the discrete ambiance of this friendly milonga there are

various combinations: men and women dancing with same-sex partners or women leading men, switching roles.

The truth is that, few things are really stable in the wide array of dance: the milongas of the last ten or fifteen years are subject to the shifting tastes of tango devotees and certain incomprehensible destinies: Which is the reason for the sky-rocketing success of certain milongas, the unbeatable persistence of a few others, and the decadence and categorical failure of many others? It is a difficult question to answer.

The most adequate floor -which must be slightly slippery but definitely not sticky-, the best disc-jockey, and the friendliest host do not guarantee the success of the venue by themselves. It is known that at an afternoon milonga in downtown Buenos Aires, opened a few years ago, the host kicks out of the place anyone who does not respect the implied rules of etiquette around the dance floor; this unfriendly attitude, however, does not reduce the attendance to the place, to the contrary. Not far away

from there, a great dance hall, sophisticated vestige of the old days, nestled on the first floor of a very traditional downtown cafeteria, is home to milongas -conducted by a different host each day- from midday to daybreak. In the same inexplicable manner that these spots become crazy fashionable, shortly after its success plummets due to equally mysterious reasons.

Other curious milonga characters are the so-called taxi-dancers, sometimes young men, but also, mature and retired gentleman that make a living by dancing tango. If at a milonga you see an impeccably-dressed mature man and experimented dancer that with undisguised resignation leads a woman who follows him with difficulty around the dance floor, you can bet he is a taxi-dancer and his occasional customer.

Contemporary milonga dancers do not belong to a certain social class or generation or a homogenous attitude towards dance. People go to a milonga to be loyal to a group of friends, to meet opposite-sex people or fill an empty life. But these reasons are always irrelevant; the most important drive is the passion for a unique and original dance.

6

Enrique Santos Discépolo

An obscure and pessimistic vision of the world is with no doubt the outstanding feature of the poetry written by Enrique Santos Discépolo, also called *Discepolín*. In his most cruel or bitter tango lyrics, such as **Qué vachaché** (Whatcha gonna do), **Yira Yira**, **Cambalache** (Second-hand shop), **Uno** (One) and **Infamia**, and also the humoristic ones as **Chorra** or **Justo el 31** tackle with deception, poignant irony and the triumph of the wrong over the right.

Discépolo, unlike any other tango poets, made his lyrics go beyond the frontier of the sentimental or dramatic recount, proper of the genre; his poetry reached, if applicable, a philosophical level, of deep skepticism.

This timid and skinny man of a big nose had manifold occupations and vocations: playwriter, actor, director, scriptwriter and, of course, composer. As he did not know how to write music, he dictated the melodies by playing them in a simple manner on the piano keyboard. Discépolo is an unusual case among tango writers, as he composed both, lyrics and music in the majority of his songs.

At the early age of twenty-five, his famous tango **Que vachaché** was premiered at a theater in Montevideo where it was noisily whistled. Three years later, in 1928, his luck changed with the success of the tango **Esta noche me emborracho** (I´m getting drunk tonight), which achieved an enormous popularity in Buenos Aires, and the rest of the country and, before long, reached Spain. Later on, that year, said success helped to rescue **Qué vachache**, interpreted by Tita Merello. Finally, in 1928 he also met Tania, a Spanish singer, who would turn out to be his wife, the adequate interpreter of his tangos and who would accompany him until the end of his days.

Although not substantial, almost Discépolo's entire work was a resounding success and his songs are among the favorite hits in the repertory of many singers.

Some months prior to Discépolo's participation in a radio program, on which he made his commitment with Peronism public, causing some troublesome distance with a lot of his friends, Homero Manzi had written a tango called **Discepolín**, with music by Anibal Troilo. The second verse of this warm portrait says the following: "I know of your long boredom and I understand what it costs to be happy, to the sound of every tango I feel your presence with your enormous talent and your nose, with your bitter, hidden tear, with your pale clown-mask, and with that sad smile that blossoms in verse and in song".

7

The "2x4" two-four time

For some unexplainable reason, the tango, that from almost a hundred years ago has been written in four-four time (namely, four pulses or times for each compass), is known as "the rhythm of the 2x4".

The news articles name it that way ninety nine times out of a hundred, even a Buenos Aires radio that broadcasts tangos all day long, is called "La 2x4". The bar of the tango and the milonga has its origins in the two-four time of the habanera, a former Cuban dance. However, as early as 1916, the tango **La cumparsita** has already been written in four-four time. Humming it and stressing the accents would be enough to recognize its rhythmic structure.

No matter what renowned tango musicians have said, from Horacio Salgán to Astor Piazzolla, trying to correct such widespread error. The misunderstanding has been imposed and is running its course successfully.

8

Nostalgia

"Remember brother, those old times…, twenty-five Aprils that will never come back! Twenty-five Aprils, who could have them back, when I see those memories I start to cry."

The nostalgia, as a deep feeling caused by an irremediable loss, appears as a tinge of a gloomy shade in tango texts. Nostalgia for the loss of a better time, for the old neighborhood, the city left behind, the childhood, the parties or the circus of early days.

But a renowned tango titled **Nostalgias** curiously evokes a very near past: "Nostalgias just to hear her laughing madly and to feel her breathing gladly like a fire right next to my mouth… Anguish, feeling lonely and abandoned, thinking someone will be standing, shortly, next to her to speak of love. My brother!".

The most remarkable fact of this tango, **Nostalgias**, is, however, its journey from Buenos Aires into an ethnic group in the Mexican state of Oaxaca. This community has adopted it and translated into their own language, currently the tango **Nostalgias** is performed in funerals ¿How do you explain this phenomenon? No-one knows; it's a mystery.

The male 9

Machismo is defined as an attitude of despise and arrogance, characterized by dominance over women. Therefore, it should be said that those who confirm that the tango is *machista* are getting it wrong. Tango men suffer for women, miss them, long for them, feel sorry for them and forgive them. It is hard to find a tango in which women are subjugated or punished.

In the extraordinary tango **Confesión** (Confession), the character did in fact mistreat his wife but with the sole purpose of drifting her away from him. As he was aware of the foreseeable collapse he would be going through, he did everything to arouse her hate and make her leave for good. It is a belated confession, as it usually is. Fatalism is a quality frequently found in the tango poetry.

The misunderstanding of labeling this tango as *machista* may be originated on the presence of a character commonly found in tango lyrics. We are referring to the *cafishio*, a lunfardo word which refers to a third-rate pimp, small scale women exploiter whose economic ambitions were modest too: just needed money to party with friends; spend on horse races and the barber's. The real males of tango-poetry have a different composition. Although the style may be diverse, they share a nobility condition: the generous losers, guys punished by life but still capable of forgiving; tough but, deep inside, sentimental, the reckless man that nothing seems to daunt but only shows their weakness before a woman, the honest men that were dragged to the abyss because of a bad woman.

These characters are the themes in tangos, such as: **Guapo y Varón** (Brave and male), **Sangre maleva** (Malevo blood), **El rey de la milonga** (The milonga king), **Ventarrón** (Strong wind), **El Tigre Millán** (Millán tiger), **Sueño Malevo** (Malevo dream), **Te llaman Malevo** (They call you Malevo). These are not arrogant characters as titles might suggest. He who is afraid of nothing, not even death, he who succumbs and cries over memories of a pair of dark eyes that someday betrayed him. He who all women gave a submissive worship ends up by surrendering to the only strong female who ignores him. The malevo who had times of victory and conquers is defeated by another man who seized his place.

A brief and perfect description of the generous male and the woman who betrays him, narrated in the first person, is found in **Milonga sentimental** (Sentimental milonga), a beautiful and very well-known tango written by Homero Manzi: The male that forgives all the insults, and even the female's abandonment without giving any explanation, and displays his nobility and tenderness by honestly showing his feelings.

From another point of view, an example of the tango man is the one with malevolent blood. The *Zurdo* Cruz Medina (The left-handed Cruz Medina), a respectable and desirable man, the archetype of the suburbs *(guapo de arrabal)*, handsome and man of action, was riddled with three bullets. The police arrive and while he is dying, the left-handed uses his last seconds to tell the policemen not to ask about the man who hurt him; a real man, should not be an informant. A man should not be a snitch, just to mention its equivalent in slang. *Delator* and *batidor* (Informant and Squealer) may be used differently depending on when the use of the slang in tango lyrics was censored.

10
The *bulín*

Let's picture the *"bulín"* as a man's fortress, a small apartment furnished with a table, some chairs, a double bed, and some basic dinnerware for a drink, a kettle and the mate, some playing cards and ash dishes. That's a typical porteño single man apartment which may be simple or more distinguished, but always with the ambience for leisure among men and for love dates, preferably, for secret lovers. It is not a place meant for practical tasks, not suitable for work or study.

In a way, the *bulín*, is a cozy dwelling place, central to bohemian life, so closely related to tango, as it is revealed in many lyrics written in its honor. The most well-known surely is **El bulín de la calle Ayacucho** (The love-nest of Ayacucho Street), inspired on a site that did actually exist. A friend had lent it to who later would be the author of the lyrics, *Negro* Celedonio Flores. He lived in the Palermo district but it was in that room of the conventillo in the centre of Buenos Aires where Celedonio used to gather with his friends.

It is known that marriage puts an end to bohemian life, and this is evidenced by the final verse of the tango **El bulín de la calle Ayacucho**, abandoned by Celedonio Flores after getting married.

11 The typical orchestra

The word "typical", so closely related to the musical tango band, means nothing more than "archetypical or traditional from a region". However, the Argentine tango typical orchestra has much more to do with an important period in the development of a style than with a place, and its distinctive sonority still rings in our ears. No doubt that the music that stemmed from the typical orchestra is the one that we still recognize as the everlasting tango music.

Tango bands' evolution over the years is due to practical reasons: the first tango musicians went performing around the bars and brothels and were not able to use more than one easy portable instrument, such as the violin, the flute and the guitar, as the primary groups used; shortly the bandoneón would be introduced. Afterwards, the piano will be incorporated at the traditional Carnival balls held in the cabaret Armenonville, and the tango will prove that it has been socially accepted and that the musicians achieved stability and better venues for their performances.

The first typical orchestras were quartets, but in the 1920's the sextets which had a piano, double-bass, two violins and two bandoneones clearly define a musical style that will continue during the next decades. The tango is no longer interpreted "on the grill" (a la parrilla) -this means without written scores nor arrangements- and this gave rise to a more cultivated and refined musical language.

Furthermore, another practical reason will appear: the modification in the number of the musicians of a typical orchestra: sound intensity becomes a need for the tumultuous traditional carnival balls which were organized in the 30's and 40's. By that time, the loudspeakers had not been created yet and the venues were much larger than theaters and cabarets, where tango was used to be performed; this was the reason why the basic number of musicians had to be multiplied.

The definite and prevailing composition of a typical orchestra until the end of the 50's was: four violins, four bandoneones, piano and double-bass. Almost fifteen years ago new typical orchestras started to emerge, formed by young musicians that, with good or bad luck, with better or worse fidelity, emulate the great typical orchestra of the golden age.

Page 54: Typical orchestra El Afronte
Page 54 & 55: Leopoldo Federico and his typical orchestra

12

The figures

The tango dance is a popular expression, another example of the long list of occidental ball dances. The tango, a century after it was born, maintains and adds a very original characteristic: the uncountable number of figures that exist or that we can imagine that may be created. There is still something to invent in this field.

Over the years, a great number of dancers, unknown, in most cases, have created tango figures and steps that did not last much or survived to date.

As it is not easy to identify the sources, there are different ways of identifying the same steps and different steps are given the same name. The poet Horacio Ferrer provides a list of steps almost vanished and so old such as *la quebrada* (the break), *la media luna* (a half-wheel), *la refalosa* (the slippery), *la tijera* (the scissors); *la estrella* (the star), *la vuelta del perro* (turn), *la corrida garabito, la rueda,* (the wheel) *la refilada* (the glimpse).

At present, not all the floor dancers know or use the steps mentioned below, but they will surely know of their existence: *la sentada* (figure in which the lady creates the illusion of sitting on, or actually mounts, the man's leg), *el giro* (turn), *el contragiro* (counter-turn), *el sangüichito* (the little bite), *el ocho adelante* (eight crossing in front), *el ocho atrás* (eight crossing behind), *el ocho cortado* (cut eights), *el balanceo* (a deep check and replace), *la arrepentida* (pentant), *el planeo* (the pivot), *la cepillada* (the brush), *los ganchos* (the hooks), *las tocadas* (the touches), *la pasadita, los boleos* (the throw), *el paso cruzado,* (the crossed step) *la bicicleta* (the bicycle), *la corrida* (short sequence of running steps), *la barrida* (the sweep), *la hamaquita* (cradle), *la cadena* (the chain), *el traspié* (cross foot), *las sacadas* (displacement of a leg or foot by the partner's leg or foot)…

Start of a turn

Sitting action

Woman´s hook

Man´s hook

High whip

Promenade
(sweetheart
walk)

Low whip

Exit or
start to
the side

Off-axis
position

Displacement

Cambalache

Those who use the absurd phrase "the Bible and the water heater" really do not know that it is extracted from the lyrics of the tango **Cambalache**. As in other legendary creations, time goes by, the author disappears and the anonymous expression survives. The huge force of this tango written by Enrique Santos Discépolo, went beyond its own limits portraying a moment and place.

The skepticism and the bitter humor expressed in **Cambalache**, released in 1935, reflect the people's mood that followed the world's stock market crash of 1929. The author confers a distinctive porteño tone to his creation. On the one hand, the incomplete or defective pronunciation of the popular speech: *Maldá* instead of *maldad* (wickedness), *estafao* instead of *estafado* (cheated), *revolcao* instead of *revolcado* (wallowed). On the other hand, the use of slang, lunfardo, i.e. *dublé* instead of *joya falsa* (fake jewelry), *chorro* instead of thief (thug for burglar), *caradura* por *desfachatado* (sassy instead of cheeky), *gil* for *tonto* (jerk instead of fool), *laburar* por *trabajar* (do a job instead of work).

Cambalache might be, perhaps, the unique example in tango poetry that introduces -together with these resources from the suburbs- a universal perspective, including a parade of important figures of the big and small history: Machiavelli; Bonaparte; Stavisky (the embezzler, not the Russian composer Stravisnky, as pronounced by some interpreters); Don Chicho, the gangster; Carnera, the boxer; and General San Martín. Discépolo expreses: *"Igual que en la vidriera irrespetuosa de los cambalaches, se ha mezclao la vida"* (Yes, just as in the junk-shop windows that show no respect for order, life is in confusion).

14

The radio

Those who know affirm that the radio and the tango were meant for each other. Until de 1940's, musicians played in cabarets and theatres and more or less lived on music. But afterwards, with the unexpected flourishing of the dance and consequently the orchestras and their singers, the radio appeared as a multiplying agent. It is simple: The musicians had to make a living from their jobs and the radio stations needed more audience, which meant bringing in more advertisers. The 40's are considered the splendorous era of the tango, due to its popularity as well as for its quality, nothing was more attractive than such a porteña and universal musical expression.

The tango was strongly identified with the radio well into the 50s, but, to date, it has never become again what it used to be.

15

Dance style

Some experts on the subject state that *"tango orillero"* (tango from the outskirts of the city) and *"tango canyengue"* are one style of dance. Others affirm that the *"tango milonguero"* does not exist. Some assure that the *"tango salón"* (ballroom tango) consists of a variety of styles which cannot be referred to as a unique thing. Finally, the *"tango nuevo"*, is not in fact "new" but the obvious result of previous evolution.

Discussions on the style are never-ending and all tango dancers have something to say on the matter. When one has the intention to clear the scene up, a few assertions are left: the *"tango canyengue"* (the word *"orillero"* seems more difficult to define as it has not been danced for a long time) it's the oldest style and now it is discretely gaining some popularity again. It is recognized through its mischievous air, cut steps that essentially rest on the music beats, the couple's heads touching, posture and the bodies quite broken. The Guardia Vieja tangos (the old guard) better suit this style.

"Tango salón" strengthened in the 1940's as more elegant and concentrated than the previously mentioned styles. There are different forms, perhaps as many as dancers,

but mostly it is identified with sliding walking and long steps, a refined musicality and a repertory of beautiful but discrete figures. The orchestra of Carlos Di Sarli would be an emblem for this style and the venues where it is better expressed are the clubs of the neighborhood of Villa Urquiza.

The so-called "tango milonguero" is characterized by its short steps and uncomplicated figures, it is danced in a closer embrace than in the "tango salón" style; and is usually played by orchestras like the D'Arienzo's or Troilo's orchestras. Some people say that it is not a style but a simple consequence or need arising from the lack of space in crowded dance-floors, at the night clubs of the centre of Buenos Aires, when the big dancehalls of older times started to disappear. That is why it is also called "tango of the City Centre".

The term "tango nuevo" refers to a dance which is widely spread among the youngest, but only for those who are willing to spend hours of practice; it is necessary to master the sudden changes of directions, displacements of the natural axis of the couple, the change of role of women, the complicated turns and other embellishments that are present in this style, sometimes dances to electronic tango pieces.

Ángel Vargas

Singers

It is quite unusual to think of the Italian lyric music as the influence on masculine tango voices of the 40's, those tenor-like voices, tuneful, that sang in a smooth and fluid-like manner. Francisco Fiorentino, Ángel D'Agostino, Roberto Rufino, Carlos Dante, Floreal Ruiz, Raúl Berón, Alberto Castillo, are just some of the many tango singers related to orchestras, not of less importance, who contributed to make tango a major art.

Edmundo Rivero, although from the same generation, differentiated himself from his contemporaries for his deep and husky voice and dull tone. For this reason, he was not accepted at the very beginning, but in the long run, he was able to impose his personal and indescribable style. His repertory included lyrics written in a suburban slang as well as in the most refined tango poetry, both styles extraordinarily interpreted by Rivero.

There are four categories of tango singers: the national singer, the *estribillistas* (refrain vocalists or *"chan-sonnier"*), the orchestra singers and the solo singer, each of them played an important role in the evolution of the tango, taking the place of an earlier style or coexisting for a short period.

The national singer initially interpreted folk rhythms, then included the first milonga tangos, and later complemented the repertory with the tango-song. The major representative of the national singer style is Carlos Gardel; other well-known interpreters are Agustin Magaldi, Ignacio Corsini and Charlo.

The refrain vocalist style, *estribillista*, was conceived from an idea of Francisco Canaro, a constant innovating conductor. The participation of the refrain vocalist in the tango orchestra started in 1924 and was somewhat weird. He appeared to sing only the bridge, *estribillo*. This was not the only discouraging aspect for the poor refrain vocalist, as he performed in noisy venues he had to be helped with small megaphones

16

Edmundo Rivero

Julio Sosa

Charlo

Alberto Castillo

to increase the sound of his voice to be heard. Progressively, the singer left behind that secondary role and started to incorporate more verses of the lyrics, and thus, increased his income. As a consequence, orchestra singers came into being.

At the beginning it involved singing longer portions of the lyrics, but shortly, the drastic change, in terms of quality, gave the opportunity to first class artists' companies, strong and unforgettable associations between orchestra and singer.

Famous names of conductors and singers appeared together in signs and marquises as a unique entity, such as D'Arienzo-Echagüe, Troilo-Fiorentino, D'Agostino-Vargas, each of them with their fans and followers.

Later, the relation changed again, many singers stepped out of the orchestra and commenced a solo singer career, with different groups. Their voices will definitely outstand. Just to mention, Roberto *"El Polaco"* Goyeneche (the Polish) and the Uruguayan Julio Sosa, two prominent figures who, among others, followed in the footsteps.

Goyeneche, who had an extensive artistic career, became both a character and a myth, a *"porteño"* through and through. His mellow voice led him to abandon melodic style songs to convert the Polish into a real "versifier". Sosa, who was born in the same year and died young in a car accident, by that time, had already attained great success with his masculine style and defiant look, in an era when tango was fading away.

73

Kisses

Two mouths get close to perform the act of kissing, but in each kiss, there is a different meaning, reflecting another mood, another emotion, another feeling. The tango poem has created all types of kisses, or almost all:

Kiss you can buy
Kiss that is given
Kiss that never come
Stolen kiss
Expected kiss (for nothing)
Kiss that wears out
Fleeting kiss
First kiss
A one happy kiss
Witch kisses
Comfort kiss
Passion kisses
Other mouth kisses
Kisses under a dim light
Painted mouth kisses
My kisses
Kissing lips that run in the wash
Flower kisses
Kisses on the eyes
Kisses that stun
Kisses that hurt
Kisses that die in the cold
Kisses getting crazy
Kisses and reproaches
Kisses and tears
Unused kisses
Furious kisses
Wise kisses
Sweet kisses
Old kisses

17

18
Corrientes street

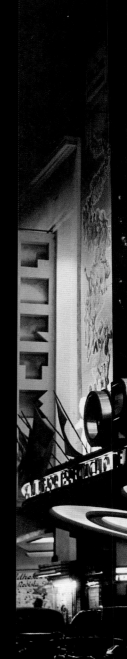

A wide and densely populated avenue since 1937. Who knows why it is called *"la Calle Corrientes"* (Corrientes street). It runs between Callao and the so-called area of el Bajo. In old times it was and, continues to be, the street that never sleeps, bustling during the day and, still hectic at night. However, the cafés featuring important tango orchestras, the bars for Bohemians and the famous cabarets Tabarís and Pigalle, are only a legend today.

No other street in Buenos Aires has been so honored through songs; the tango poets created different images of the Corrientes street. From the distance, as in **Anclao en París** (Anchored in Paris) it is the place which distance makes more beautiful:

"How must have changed your Corrientes street!
Suipacha, Esmeralda, your very own suburb!
Somebody has told me that you're flourishing
and a set of streets run in diagonal
you don't know how much I wish to see you!
Here I am stuck, without money or faith."

The beautiful tango **Tristezas de la Calle Corrientes** (Corrientes street blues) provides a different vision:

"What a sad paleness your lights have!
Your signs burdened by dreams!
And your posters...only cardboard laughter! (…)
Market of the sad pleasures...
Cambalache of caresses hanging on an illusion!
(…) Men sold you... betrayed you like Jesus, and the
dagger of the Obelisk makes you bleed, endlessly."

Corrientes is also depicted in the shady colors of the ruins in homonymous tango:

"Corrientes, street of vices one night you get me drunk, you gave me so much poison that nobody can resist your fatal lights."

This street has also been portrayed with the joyful colors of sin in the tango **A media luz** (Everything half-lighted):

"Corrientes three-four-eight, second floor, elevator; there are no doormen or neighbors; inside, cocktail and love. (....) On afternoons, tea with pastries; at night, tango and love. On Sundays, tea dancing; on Mondays, emptiness. There is everything in the little house: pillows and sofas; like in a drugstore... cocó, carpets muffling the sound and a table set for love."

When Carlos Gardel's remains were brought to Buenos Aires, after his fatal accident in Medellín in June 1935, his body laid in state at the Luna Park stadium, on the extreme of Corrientes street, and was taken to La Chacarita cemetery, on the other side of the city. Corrientes had been widened but it would officially be opened the following year, but instead, an unexpected and impressive baptism occurred at such popular ceremony. Along seventy blocks, ten thousand people gathered and attended this funeral procession. Scratches of the old houses of the old narrow Corrientes street were still visible, though now it showcased new bars and theatres. The street would no longer be the same; however, tango would continue to live there.

19

La cumparsita

A curious tango lover some years ago decided to compile all different versions of **La cumparsita** tango (The little parade) that had been recorded throughout history. When he reached version number two hundred, he got exhausted and, presuming that he was facing a never-ending task, he gave up. Surely, there is no other tango song with so many sound recordings or that has been played in movies so much, not necessarily argentine movies, than this one: actor William Holden danced **La cumparsita** with Gloria Swanson in **El ocaso de una vida (Sunset Boulevard)**; Jack Lemmon did his version disguised as woman in **Una Eva y dos Adanes (Some Like it Hot)**; Woody Allen chose some passages for **Días de radio (Radio Days)** and **Alice**, and Gene Kelly made his Hollywood style version of **La cumparsita** in the musical film **Leven anclas (Anchors Aweigh)**.

La cumparsita was composed in 1916 by a young Uruguayan student called Gerardo Matos Rodríguez, at first with no lyrics. Later on, some legal issues derived from the lyrics written for its melody and, as a result instrumental versions of this piece prevailed.

One of the most popular versions is the one recorded by Juan D'Arienzo's orchestra in 1948 which, he assured, had sold 18 million copies.

There are two facts to mention: the first one, at every milonga in Buenos Aires, since the forties to date, either at neighborhood clubs or city ballrooms **La cumparsita** is the last dance played. That means that the evening is over and the remaining couples hurry to dance the last piece.

The other really extravagant fact is that in Turkey wedding couples at their party dance **La cumparsita** instead of the habitual and universal waltz.

Where does the title come from? Matos Rodríguez was part of a *cumparsa* of students (Lunfardo word that denotes a group of people that attends the Carnival festivals dressed in a similar fashion). Matos frequented a bar in Montevideo and its Italian waiter used to greet him with a "here comes the *cumparsita*!".

20

The improvisation

The music is about to play and the tango dancer is ready to groove the dancing floor with his partner; but certainly, nothing has been planned beforehand, how it will commence, nor which is the step combination and, far less, how the whole tango would be like. This is because the improvisation, a mastered skill, rules the tango dance.

The floor dancer holds a treasure full of steps and figures, and during the three minutes that the musical piece lasts, he picks out the steps and figures what suits best to his ability, knowledge, experience and inspiration. Be careful, a fantasy dancer, who improvises a great number of figures, may fall into overelaboration if he lacks musicality. Quite the opposite occurs with the one who has a limited repertory of steps, perhaps he may have a stronger connection to the music and with his eventual partner. This is the untouchable richness of the dance.

The humor

Certainly the tango does not have a bent for humor, but, proportionally speaking, among the small samples of comic tangos lyrics, there are extraordinary works. We can mention **Chorra** (Thief), tango which narrates the misadventures of a butcher who is tricked by a skillful and beautiful fibber. **Gorda** (Fat) recounts a woman's mourn who, as she gains weight, she loses her lover. **Un baile a beneficio** (Charity ball), describes the list of guests, of every kind and look, who will attend a charity ball given to raise money for a man who was put in prison for stealing.

In this short listing the milonga **Amablemente** (Kindly) cannot be missed out. A short story masterpiece, interpreted extraordinarily by Edmundo Rivero. Ivan Diez, the author, uses fourteen lines in the Spanish classical sonnet form to write in the most authentic slang. In this short poem Diez clearly provides a setting, presents the characters, creates a climax of slight tension and saves the black humor for the end.

The story narrates that a guy arrives at his home and finds his wife in the arms of another man; he doesn't get angry with his rival and invites him to leave (saying: "in these cases, men are not responsible"). He requests her wife to prepare and brew *mate*, frightened as she was, she obeys; then he lights a cigarette and starts talking about trivial things, after that, calmly and kindly he stabs her to death (34 times).

22

Homero Manzi

Barrio de tango (Neighborhood tango), **Sur** (South), **Malena**, **Romance de barrio** (Neighborhood romance), **Milonga sentimental**: the mere listing of this handful of titles written by Homero Manzi would be enough to understand the dimension and implication of his poetry work, evidenced only through tango lyrics, definitely, a breath of fresh air in those days.

Manzi (1907), Homero Manzioni, as he was truly named, born in Añatuya -later re-named by him Añamía- in the province of Santiago del Estero, was and is an im-mensely popular poet who did not resort to either slang or everyday speech expres-sions. Farm and urban motifs are present in his work which is tinged with nostalgia for things and people lost.

The neighborhood of Pompeya is described in his most famous piece, **Sur** (South) (is there any Argentine who hasn't sung Sur, somehow or other, in his life?). Here, Manzi makes use of the distinctive enumeration resource present in his poetry. From the first verse the author resorts to enumeration, simple and touching tool through which he describes a time and a place: the crossing of two streets, the name of the neighborhood, a corner, a job, the smells, the girlfriend and the simple things in his memories; only the evocative of emotion appears in the last line of this verse.

"Old San Juan and Boedo streets corners,
the sky Pompeya and further on, the floods.
Your loose hair of a bride in my memory
and your name floating in the farewell.
The blacksmith's corner, mud and pampa,
your house, your sidewalk, and the ditch
and a scent of weeds and alfalfa
that fills the heart all over again."

The tango **Sur** has music by Anibal Troilo, with whom Manzi created one of the most valuable couples of tango authors; not because of the number of pieces -which were only six- but for its value and transcendence. Five of them, belonging to the 1940's, were to become a milestone of the tango repertoire: the before mentioned **Sur** (South), **Barrio de tango** (Tango neighborhood), **Ché bandoneón** (Hey, bandoneón), **Romance de barrio** (Neighborhood romance) and **Discepolín**. Manzi wrote motivating milonga lyrics, enriching this rhythm of rural origins which was somewhat under estimated.

Together with pianist and composer Sebastián Piana, he wrote famous classics, such as **Milonga triste** (Sad milonga), **Milonga sentimental** (Sentimental milonga) and **Milonga del novecientos** (Milonga of 900). The waltz **Paisaje** (Landscape) is also the result of the extraordinary couple Piana-Manzi. Manzi also wrote the lyrics for other unforgettable waltzes, such as **Desde el alma** (From the soul) and **Esquinas porteñas** (Corners of Buenos Aires).

Homero Manzi's romantic bent, derived from his early fondness for Ruben Darío's literary work, was reflected in beautiful lyrics: **Fruta amarga** (Sour fruit), **Torrente** (Torrent), **Después** (After), and **Ninguna** (No other). In the tango **Fuimos** (We were), the character expresses in a brilliant manner the devastating separation; because at the same time he is asking his lover to leave, he is shouting her name aloud. The splendid piece **Tal vez será su voz** (It might be her voice) with music by Lucio Demare, was censored in 1943 by the military government. The original title was **Tal vez será el alcohol** (It might be the alcohol) and was changed to **Tal vez será su voz.** The word "alcohol" and any other phrases suggesting drunkenness were eliminated.

Homero Manzi died at the early age of 44. Through his lifetime, with steady intensity and undergoing turbulent personal moments, he indulged in journalism, teaching and films, and also got involved in trade unions and politics.

Milonga Sentimental

MILONGA

Estrenada con gran éxito por las tiples Paquita Garzón y Rosita Contreras y los chansoniers Casaravilla y García, en la Revista "El Sueño del Peludo", que se representa en el Teatro Casino.

Letra de	Música de
H. MANZI	**SEBASTIAN PIANA**
	637 B

Unico editor autorizado
HECTOR N. PIROVANO
Pasco 1440   Buenos Aires
Argentina
De la Asoc. Arg. de Editores

23

Tango championships

Any tango dance floor is a natural competition place: from the gentleman and lady that dance a finely erotic *minué* at Versailles palace to the languid couple that rocks to the rhythm of the *danzón* in a public square of the Mexican city of Veracruz, the social dance is an involuntary (but sometimes also voluntary) demonstration of distinction, ability, inventive, seduction and grace. From there, to the straight competence, directed by certain rules, there is just one step.

The tango dance championship has its own history. Nourished by amateur dance couples, the championship also occasionally has launched professional artists. Probably, we should talk about "dance contest" and not "championship", because this word has a certain sport connotation. However, it is a long-accepted term. It was used in that famous tango championship at the Luna Park, in 1951, when the public acclaimed as winners a young couple of milonga dancers, the later famous Juan Carlos Copes and María Nieves Rego, in front of an audience of 10 thousand people.

Anyway, a tango championship, regardless of its scale, if it's worth for something is to discover or reveal the treasures that underlie a popular cultural expression, this term used in the noblest and most genuine sense.

24

The alcohol

Neither raising glasses nor glasses clinking as symbol and expression of joyful celebration are commonly seen in tango. Rivers of champaign, wine, rum, cane, staple, wormwood and ajenjo flow in torrents through tango lyrics, to drown the pain caused by loss and betrayal; to forget the insults to indignity or notice the overwhelming fall of a man or a woman. Other situations also call for some alcohol: In the tango

Esta noche me emborrracho (I'm getting drunk tonight) written by Enrique Santos Discépolo, the central character meets by chance an old sweetheart of his, coming out of a nightclub. She was the woman who some time before had driven him crazy, made him betray his friends, steal food from his mother and even let his friends abandon him. Now he finds her lonely, old, thin, with crooked legs, badly-dyed. A wreck. "This encounter made me feel so bad" and the wretch finally says: "That if I think it through I'll get poisoned, tonight I'll get drunk, very drunk so I won't think".

The tango also includes some boozers, just for the sake of drinking:

"Hey buddy, give me another rum I'm drinking without rhyme or reason I don't do it because of love. That's an old excuse or because I want to elude my heart. I'm not stunned by bad memories I don't have to forget a betrayal I drink because I do... 'cause I'm a complete lush! To me there's always an occasion to drink." (Tango **De puro curda** (A complete lush) by Olmedo and Aznar.)

Finally, alcohol can inspire the most beautiful poetry, as Enrique Cadícamo used to portray a couple that meets for a moment and for last time together. **Los mareados** (Dizzy) with music by Juan Carlos Cobián: "Crazy, almost on fire, I found you drinking, lovely and fierce; imbibing, and in the din of champagne, laughing insanely, so as not to cry. Painful it was to find you, since when I saw you I saw your eyes shining with an electrical glow, your lovely eyes that I adored so much. Yes, tonight my friend, we're getting drunk I don't care if people mock us and they say that we're just dizzy!".

25

The pure woman

The thought goes back in search of the lost girlfriend; this is one of the most interpreted themes in the tango repertoire, as expressed in **Gricel**. Written in the first-person, he recalls her with regret, knowing that he should never have thought about her. Gricel seemed too good for this man who, we suspect, was not worthy of her.

Other kisses are not enough to forget her. The past will often be the place where the innocent girlfriend would live, lost forever, and the famous tango **Gricel** expresses it in an admirable way.

But since the threat of losing innocence permanently lurks in the universe of tango -as other lyrics narrate so well- the wise advice from **Atenti pebeta** (Careful, babe!) is welcomed, it lectures on how to continue through the right path.

It is not clear if it is an uncle, a parent or a good friend who gives these tips: lengthen the skirt, tie your hair back firmly, say goodbye to creams and make-up; at tea time, drink milk with vanilla cookies or chocolate with *churros* (crullers). And if necessary, have a gun at hand to kill the first guy that cheats you.

Astor
Piazzolla

Astor Piazzolla, with his challenging
and provocative style that characterized him, once said that all he knew,
from the musical point of view, he had
learnt from his French teacher Nadia
Boulanger, during an intense year of
study in Paris. This was not completely
true. Certainly, in his way of composing,
when he initiates his more innovative
phase, there is a clear influence in the
use of counterpoints and harmonies of
Johann Sebastian Bach, who had also
studied with Nadia Boulanger.

However, Piazzolla's music had also
been influenced by the well-known Hun-
garian composer Béla Bartók, American
jazz and, of course, the tango itself.

Astor Piazzolla was born in Mar del Plata
in 1921 and performed the music of the
Río de la Plata region in an exceptional
manner. At the age of nine he received
a bandoneón as gift from his father and
for a long time he only played classical
music. The Piazzolla family established
in New York in 1924 as modest immigrants and Astor lived there almost all
his childhood and part of his youth.

A very curious story of those old days
seems to speak about destiny: Piazzolla's

father was a barber and an amateur wood carver; he greatly admired Carlos Gardel and when Gardel arrived in New York he sent his son with a wooden carved gaucho holding a guitar. The boy went into Gardel's apartment through the fire stairs.

-Who are you? -asked Gardel, who was with Alfredo Le Pera.

-I am an Argentine kid who lives here.

-How wonderful!

"And when I added that I played the bandoneón -recalled Piazzolla- he almost died. We shared breakfast and had some café latte and a pudding with raisins. I accompanied him for almost a year. I was his translator when he went to important department stores to buy clothes." Later, Astor participated in a small role as a newspapers seller in **El día que me quieras** (The day you love me) that Gardel filmed in New York.

Piazzolla is the world most famous tango composer and his work is executed by important international orchestras. However, he began his professional career playing in unknown cafés and dark suburban clubs.

By the end of 1930's he was incorporated to Anibal Troilo's orchestra, of whom he would later be his arranger. Troilo tutored Piazzolla, but also trimmed his wings so that he will make danceable music and not drift away from the popular taste.

Astor formed his own orchestra in 1946, and in 1955 created his major enterprise: Octeto de Buenos Aires. The creation of this octet, which many experts regard as the artistic zenith of his career, is a turning point in Piazzolla's trajectory, something already outlined in previous years.

The new approach and innovation of rhythm structures and counterpoints caused a savage rejection in the tango environment; the disqualifying phrase "This is not tango" was constantly repeated and widely spread; however, they decisively influenced post-Piazzolla music, which until today seems not to be able to get rid of that statement.

And by the way, with so many influences, where is the true tango in Piazzolla's work? A question which would give rise to extensive arguments; however, it allows a tentative and partial response: first, the distinctive tango sound of the bandoneón; second, the formation of its most celebrated groups, which in general maintained the archetypical orchestra composition.

101

27

Men lead, women follow

The first time one is in front of a tango dancing couple on a dance floor and he clearly knows that what he is watching is not a series of set steps prepared beforehand, would not hesitate to task: "thanks to what mysterious agreement can this couple move so harmoniously?". Because the truth is that both make individual steps and figures simultaneously; men can hold women while they turn; women may stop while her partner makes a figure with his feet and other countless elements.

A singularity of tango, a substantial feature that has not changed for over 100 years, is that the male dancer uses his chest and arm to lead the movements, the steps and figures of his partner during the dance.

That mysterious agreement that surprises those who have never danced arises from the subtle "mark" that the man prints on the woman and her immediate precise response: neither too rushed or with excessive delay.

Some unwise feminists argue that, this, say, female "dependency", makes tango a male dance, and entails a certain relationship of domination and subjugation. That is a mistake: When a man dances really well, his most important objective is to display the beautifulness of the lady dancing with him.

28

The lyrics

Tango, as other genres of folk songs, talks about lucky and unlucky love, losses, deception, loneliness, childhood and memories. But its repertoire is not reduced to such romantic issues. On the contrary, it seems that everything is possible when narrated through a tango: the neighborhood, friendship, football, courage, overweight, work, social claim, carnival, the port and the sea, cafés, bar and drinks, landscapes, cigarette, dance and dancers. And even more: Tango poetry has tackled with an original theme like horse races, a hobby and passion of the *porteños* that is still alive.

Not fewer than twenty tango lyrics have been written about the world of horse racing, certainly, the most famous and popular is **Por una cabeza** (By a nose (of a horse)) interpreted by Carlos Gardel. It is a confession made by a man trapped by gambling on horse races (the *"burros"*) -and the love of a woman- an ap-

proach that also appears with a more humorous tone in the well-known tango **Palermo**: "Damn you, Palermo! You've dried me up and made me sick, badly-dressed and without a bite to eat, because on Sundays I drain all my money on the horses at the *Hache Nacional* (horse race venue). I choke on *"La Verde"* (a horse race magazine) looking for the winner, and studying the pedigree, and despite the efforts, I through away at the betting box all my monthly pay".

Two tangos were written to honor Ireneo Leguisamo, a legendary jockey nicknamed "the Octopus": one of them titled after him and another simply called **Salvame Legui** (Save me Legui). The first one has a moderate epic tone: "There is no doubt; it is the wrist and the serene and enormous heart which succeed by the nose with great style and precision. He takes the horses to the victory with such professional skill that he is distinguished with glory, a mixture of awe and admiration".

The second tango is a desperate shout: "Save me Legui, save me Legui! that I bet 1000 and 1000, and if it happens this man is saved!... bye bye ponies, I flee to Paris, save me Legui, save me Legui, my dear Octopus, please, bring it close, let him go as soon as I step on the grandstand".

29

The café

A century ago, at today's Congreso neighborhood, there used to be a famous café called *El Estribo*. This place has played host to important tango musicians, which later became part of the history: The trio Firpo-Arolas-Roccatagliata; the quartet formed by Francisco Canaro, Vicente Greco, Prudencio Aragón and Vicente Pecci; and the Gardel-Razzano Duo. Cafés in Buenos Aires were, for a long time, extraordinary places to listen to tango and when this custom faded away, they continued to be the *porteños* prominent spot for gathering. In this way, cafés are reflected on tango poetry as a shelter for men -usually criticized by wives and girlfriends- where they spend extended hours arguing about politics and sports, talking about women, or playing dice or pool. There is a very typical expression, "the guys from the café", referring to the group of friends that do not belong to the family circle. The cafés also used to be, and usually are, a place to discuss and close business issues. Legendary tango dancer Benito Bianquet, nicknamed "El

Cachafaz", was a frequent visitor at café *El Estaño*, located at the corner of Talcahuano and Corrientes streets; there, at his habitual table, which he called "my office", he dealt with his business, gathered with friends and received anybody that wished to see him. Not less legendary is café *Los Angelitos* in the corner of Rivadavia and Rincón. At its early beginnings, it was frequented by workers and later it became the favorite venue of *payadores* (those who perform *payadas* -improvised folk songs). Carlos Gardel and José Razzano signed their first recording contract there and other major tango figures were regular customers too.

Nowadays, there is a café of the same name at that same corner, although devoted to another tango. It is not the same venue honored in the tango composed by Razzano and Cátulo Castillo, surrounded by an aureole of nostalgia: "I evoke you, lost in the life and entangled in smoke threads, in front of a pleasing memory that I smoke and a black cup of coffee. Rivadavia and Rincón!... Old corner of the old friendship that returns, flirting its grey on the table that is meditating in its yesterday nights". (**Café de los Angelitos**)

30

The bandoneón

The bandoneón was invented in Germany in 1835 in a rudimentary form; it was brought to the Río de la Plata river area towards the mid-19th century. Once it was incorporated by the first tango groups, in those days the trios were made up of flute, violin and guitar, it gradually started to assert itself as the most identifiable sonority of the genre. The flute with its cheerful embellishments was displaced by the newcomer and it is presumed that the bandoneón changed the tango's personality, taking it from that jumping rhythm of the first Milonga-Tangos to the paused speed and deep character later adopted.

It is certainly a hypothesis, but nothing unreasonable: the bandoneón is a difficult instrument to master thus intuitive musicians, with no study, had to play it in a rather more delayed tempo than what had been usual until then.

There is a question worth asking: why is it that the sound of the bandoneón is so intimately connected to the distinctive complaint and the lament of the tango? A possible explanation would be that this wind instrument allows the air to be exhaled with a variety of durations and nuances; the resulting sounds have thus a strange animal-like quality; or if you prefer, human-like.

31

Poets

The limits of poetry are hard to precise when we step into the territory of popular genres; we all know many songs with inspired lyrics, however, we still do not dare to refer to them as poems.

As regards the tango, this does not seem to be a topic at issue; it has had the capacity to produce real poems and authentic poets. Perhaps, it is the other way round: the authentic poets were the ones who gave tango a portion of their wisdom.

The truth is that tango poetry, the most prominent one, was nurtured or influenced by several trends of the so-called classical literature while it continued to serve the cause of a popular genre.

The notorious names of tango poets form a list that nobody would object: José María Contursi, Cátulo Castillo, Enrique Cadícamo, Homero Expósito, Celedonio Flores; for others, also Francisco García Jiménez and Héctor Pedro Blomberg. Of course, Homero Manzi and Enrique Santos Discépolo, should be added to this list, but they are discussed separately in this book.

When Pacual Contursi wrote the lyrics of **Mi noche triste** (My sad night) -which Carlos Gardel sang in 1917, collaborating with its enormous acceptance- he opened the path to a new possibility in tango: telling stories within the short text of a song. Some academics think that Contursi is a poet and to others he is only a lyricist because his literary resources were very basic. But later, other creators with education and literary ambitions emerged and continued the path of the tango-song with real poetic soundness. Therefore, beautiful and suggestive metaphors were mixed and merged into the best music of its time.

The most recurrent themes in tango, as already mentioned, are love, loss, betrayal, disappointment, guilt. José María Contursi, Pascual's son, was the tango poet par

Page 116: Homero Expósito

excellence. He wrote some of his most famous tangos with music by Mariano Mores: **Gricel**, **Cristal**, and **En esta tarde gris** (On this grey afternoon).

Celedonio Flores portrayed, in a very rich form, characters and situations of the life in Buenos Aires, mastering a neat *lunfardo*. He is the composer of well-known lyrics, such as **Mano a mano** (We're even), **Margot**, **El bulín de la calle Ayacucho** (The love-nest of Ayacucho street), **Corrientes y Esmeralda** and **Viejo smoking** (Old tuxedo).

Enrique Cadícamo, who lived almost for a hundred years, displayed throughout his life a wide range of literary recourses and narrative selections. It is worth mentioning **Muñeca brava** (Mad doll), **De todo te olvidas** (You forget it all), **Nieblas del Riachuelo** (Fog in the Riachuelo), **Los mareados** (Dizzy) and **Anclao en París** (Anchored in Paris).

Cátulo Castillo, a nostalgy poet, has used, not by chance, the word "last" in several titles of his works: **El último cafiolo** (The last cafiolo), **La última curda** (The last booze), **El último café** (The last coffee) or **El último farol** (The last streetlamp). Other tangos composed by him are **Tinta roja** (Red ink), **Caserón de tejas** (with a waltz tempo) (The big house with a tiled roof), **Café de los Angelitos**.

Homero Expósito was initially rejected because of his unusual metaphors, though he insisted with them. He worked jointly with most prominent authors of the 40's and some of his celebrated works are **Naranjo en flor** (Orange tree in blossom), **Percal** (Percale), **Yuyo verde** (Green weed), **Tristezas de la Calle Corrientes** (Sadness of Corrientes street), **Al compás del corazón** (At the heart beat).

In the last two decades two composers of tango poetry have stood out. One of them is Horacio Ferrer, broadly known for his **Balada para un loco** (Ballad for a madman), with music by Astor Piazzolla, with whom Ferrer worked in collaboration for over twenty years. "The Piazzolla of the Lyrics", according to José Gobello, innovates thematically and aesthetically through his opera **María de Buenos Aires** the most staged Latin-American play in the world, as well as many of his famous lyrics. The other important figure is Eladia Blázquez, who also wrote the music of her own tangos. Blázquez's also features a curious mixture: disappointment and hopeful humanism. **Sueño de barrilete** (Kite's dream) and **El corazón al sur** (The heart to the south) are her most popular tangos.

Horacio Ferrer

32

Milonga
and Waltz

Together with the tangos, although in a lower proportion, waltzes and milongas complete the sonoric atmosphere of an entire ballroom, offering their own shades. The milonga -do not confuse it with the name of the dancing hall- is the most primitive rhythm within the genre. In other words: nowadays the milonga is similar to the tango of the very beginnings. The milonga is vivacious and cheerful, even the slower ones, because unhurried milongas exist. The typical two beat compass shares many figures with the tango, but it also has its exclusive forms. During the last decade the traspié (cross foot) became stylish again; a very complicated milonga step that drove the enthusiastic followers of this rhythm wild.

The waltz, as it is known, is a ballroom dance born in Vienne at the end of the 18th century. The waltz that the milongueros of Buenos Aires adopted under the name *vals cruzado* (crossed waltz) maintains the three-beat rhythm, but it is danced using quick tango steps, like an impetuous flow that never stops. When tango is danced, the dancers often wear a solemn and concentrated face. The *vals cruzado* shows a blissful devotion and the milonga an unrestrained joy.

Tita Merello

33

Song interpreters

Women may be beautiful or not; extravagant or frugal; with miserable or happy lives. The most important tango women interpreters do not represent a unique type of woman, not for their lineage, style or its vocal characteristics. In a short period, from 1986 to 1913, and due to some weird planetary alignment, the birth of those who would be tango celebrities occurred; figures of great singularity that paved the way for women to step into this genre.

Each of them shined in a different way, they were the expression of a definite unique phenomenon. Today, do their voices sound old-fashioned? Is the way they sing archaic? Such prejudice existed some time ago, but, nowadays, it cannot be sustained. Listening to them would be enough:

Rosita Quiroga (1986) was born in La Boca and even when she was a well-known artist and earned a lot of money, the way she talked and the popular and slang vocabulary used in her repertory still represented her suburban origins. Her high-pitched and low voice, not much educated, usually accompanied by guitars, has an original and moving expressivity. She commenced her career early and she decided to retire young.

Azucena Maizani (1902) was born in a modest home, worked in a sewing workshop, and then in silent movies and the *revista*, a musical variety show. One day she approached Francisco Canaro to take an audition for singer. Canaro hired her and renamed her Azabache. The popularity of the also called Ñata Gaucha, who used to dress up as a man, *malevo* or *gaucho*, grew rapidly in 1923, comparable to Carlos Gardel's popularity. Although her voice was not strong, her performances had a real dramatic character. She lived a life full of unfortunate love and painful events. She composed beautiful tangos that are still sung and died penniless and forgotten.

Mercedes Simone (1904): For many people, she was the most remarkable complete female tango singer. She was a beautiful woman with a refined and sentimental style and impeccable diction. She began her career accompanying her husband, guitarist and singer Pablo Rodríguez, in small tours around the province of Buenos Aires. She settled in Buenos Aires, where she started her professional career in the most important cafés of that time. Rosita Quiroga discovered her at the Chantecler and recommended her to the Víctor label. In 1933 Mercedes Simone, together with her colleagues Libertad Lamarque, Tita Merello and Azucena Maizani, took part in the film **Tango!**, the first Argentine sound film, singing for the first time, her own song **Cantando** (Singing).

Tita Merello (1904) had an obscure birth and spent her childhood in an asylum. She worked as a *bataclana* -name taken from a Buenos Aires theatre of those times called Ba-ta-clán- and later as a *vedette*, reaching her first success in the play **Leguisamo solo**. Her voice was not so good nor was it particularly tuned, but her "scruffy" personality, strengthened the character of her interpretations and special mischievous and humorous tangos and milongas. For almost twenty years, she devoted herself fully to theatre and movies, but in 1954 had a successful return by recording with the Orchestra of Francisco Canaro.

Ada Falcón (1905) was perhaps the only artist of this generation that could be described as "diva". Pushed

by a tenacious mother, she made her singing debut at the age of five; by the time she was twenty, she had already recorded with the Orchestra of Osvaldo Fresedo. Admired for her beauty and fascinating green eyes; her success grew and so did her whims. Her way of singing, which may sound a little affected today, had a mournful and emotive character, really personal. She experienced a long and complicated relationship with Francisco Canaro and was artistically associated with him too; the ending of this relationship also put an end to her career. In 1942 she confined herself to a convent and lived there until her death.

Libertad Lamarque (1908) came from a home of anarchist ideas and intellectual and artistic concerns. At the age of eighteen she made her first professional appearance in a comedy sketch, shortly after, she appeared on radio and almost immediately began recording for the Víctor label. Her soprano very high-pitched voice was clear, expressive and with a perfect tuning. Her career was long and exceptionally successful in radio, theatre and film. She took part in many films in Argentina and Mexico, where she settled after a famous argument with Eva Perón. She has more than four hundred recordings.

Nelly Omar (1913) is a contemporary singer, on the edge of the first decade of the third millennium. She is a wonderfully equipped interpreted, devoted herself equally to folk music and tango repertories. Homero Manzi, had been her lover for many years, he wrote for her the famous tango **Malena**. She was forbidden for many years due to her commitment to Peronism.

Libertad Lamarque

126

34

Paris

For several years, on a small esplanade on the banks of the Seine and not far from the famous Latin neighborhood, dancers and curious onlookers get together to tango on Sunday afternoons during spring and summer. Parisian milongueros, who reproduce the figures and styles, as well as the twitches of their *porteño* fellows, dance outdoors at this beautiful and peaceful spot. The recorded music is the same that is played at any milonga in Buenos Aires. Although the Seine Milonga is the most original for its location, it is not the only one in the city. Any compulsive aficionado could dance tango in Paris any day of the week if he wishes to do so. There is no other place in the world, including the countless cities that contracted the tango fever during the last few decades, more entitled than Paris to boast a legitimacy of origin. When the tango arrived in Paris in 1913, it was enthusiastically accepted by the French high society and returned to Buenos Aires with an aura of respectability that it would never loose. Both these cities were so knotted together that a well-known night club in those days promoted itself as "a cabaret made to measure for Argentine millionaires". It was called Princesse and had been renamed *El Garrón*, a lunfardo (slang) name of brothel origin: *Garrón* is the free favor that a prostitute offers to the man that she likes. The owners of this place of ambiguous name were the Pizarro brothers, two Argentine tango musicians. *El Garrón* was one of the most famous cabarets of those days not only for its clientele but also for the quality of its music. Many decades later, at the downtown neighborhood of Les Halles a new spot opened its doors and would gain a mythical relevance: *Trottoirs de Buenos Aires*. Contrary to **Tango Argentino** show, which premiered in Paris two years later and boosted the renaissance of tango, *Trottoirs* was mainly a musical phenomenon, partly promoted by Argentine painters, musicians and writers living in Paris. Among them was Julio Cortázar, a kind of patron of *Trottoirs*, who wrote the lyrics of a tango for this venue.

There is a neighborhood in Paris that particularly identifies with tango: Montmartre, the place of choice for artists and center of Paris bustling nightlife. The same-name tango exaggerates such identification between Buenos Aires and Paris by affirming that the porteño neighborhood of Boedo is just a step away from Montmartre and wonders naively: "Montmartre, who made you Argentine, with your mill and your faubourg?".

The well-known **Anclao en París** (Anchored in Paris) is placed at the opposite point of view. This song, wonderfully interpreted by Carlos Gardel, sings to Buenos Aires as an expatriate would do. The character looks through the window at the snow falling down on Montmartre roofs and painfully misses the city that he had left behind ten years before.

Another tango, not less famous, follows the steps of a cheerful French girl that leaves her Paris neighborhood to follow an Argentine handsome fellow, presumably a cheater, who leaves her to her fate. The unforgettable **Madame Ivonne**, it is about her that we are talking, is stuck in Buenos Aires forever, far away from her homeland and from the girl that she used to be.

Page 129:
Seine Milonga

The lunfardo

Originally the lunfardo was the slang spoken among thieves in Buenos Aires. Rapidly this slang was extended and was enhanced with immigrants' speech, deformed words due to pronunciation difficulties, and other habits such as inversion of the syllabic order of a word, *vesre* (metathesis of *revés*, which means back to front). The lunfardo is like a land in constant movement; it expands with new terms and is reduced at the same time, some terms have faded away and others persisted for a long time. The tango raised this street language to a poetic level and those many words used in lyrics to refer to women and men, trades, categories and different characteristics became everlasting.

Regarding the female terms, everybody knows that *mina* refers in a broad sense to women, as well as *paica* and *sofaifa*, although rarely used. The terms *papusa, budín* and *biscuí* only refer to beautiful women whilst *loro* and *bagayo* refer to ugly ones. *Percanta* refers to a concubine woman; *chirusa, china* and *griseta* to girls of humble condition and, the sweet expression *milonguita* refers to the young women that work in night venues for fun.

As to the male terms we can mention the popular term *compadrito* which in the old days meant "young man of the suburbs" and afterwards it was simply used as synonymous to *fanfarrón* (braggart). The *malevo* was a bully and troublemaker; the *taita*, a brave guy and the *taura* a daring man. *Caferata, canfinflero, cafishio* and *cafiolo* a man that lives on one or more women or prostitute; *pituco* and *shusheta*, wealthy, elegant and refined men; as well as *bacán*, which has its equivalent in *vesre: camba*.

Afano: Robbery, swindle, cheat / overpay. Synonyms in lunfardo: *curro, chafar, chorear:* to swipe (thief). "Hey, Tango, hey you steal me the clothes, the success and the faith".

Arrugar: To get frightened, scared; to chicken out.

Atorranta: Prostitute, hooker.

Atorrante: Lazy, layabout. Derived from the verb *torrar,* which means to sleep. / Cheeky, sassy. "*Atorrante!*... Aren't you ashamed when people see you go by, what people think of you and constantly talk about you".

Avanzar: To make a move on somebody, used generally for love affairs.

Avivar: To wise up; realize about something unnoticed / to be brave.

Bagayo: Frampy, very ugly person, unpleasant look / baggage, luggage.

Batidor: Snitch, informer, fink, somebody who accuses other in secret and carefully. Synonym for accuser, *buchón* in lunfardo.

Berreta: Cheap, of bad quality.

Bife: Slap

Bocho: Head / Very intelligent person.

Bodrio: Very boring. Synonym in lunfardo for *embole*, dreary.

Bondi: Bus.

Buchón: Accuser, informer; somebody who accuses in secret and carefully. Synonym for snitch, *batidor* in lunfardo.

Careta: False, that pretends to be something different from reality. "One must be more than *careta* to pretend to be a refined while she is sick and without prescription and has two starving kids".

Compadre: Braggart. Man with an attitude of a tough guy. "No doubt, you've been self-deceived by your features of *compadre*". / Co-parent, man who is not part of the family but is respected as if he were / Friend, mate.

Curro: Robbery / to cheat / to over pay. Synonyms in lunfardo: *afanar, chafar, chorear* (to swipe).

Chabón: Young man, usually used among teens to address each other. Derived from the word *chambón;* very common people (according the Spanish Royal Academy -Real Academia Española-).

Chafar: To steal / to steal surreptitiously, taking advantage of lack of attention. Synonyms in lunfardo: *afanar, curro, chorear (de chorro)*. Swipe

Chamuyo: Lies, far-fetched excuses. Synonym in lunfardo: *sanata*. Speech usually used by a man to make compliments or talk into a woman.

Chorro: Thief, somebody who robs or steals. "The jet plane was invented and the "*chorro*" escapes on a jet". / Somebody that wins something not deserved.

Deschavar: Discover, reveal. "Let me die in peace, without revealing his name that a man to be a man cannot be a snitch".

Despelote: Mess, muddle, chaos

Embole: Boring. Synonym in lunfardo: *bodrio*.

Empilchar: To dress up, to dress elegantly. Derived from Lunfardo: *pilcha:* clothes. "*Empilchada* lipstick mouth, tooth brush polished nails".

Fajar: Beat, to beat violently.

Feca: (Methathesis of *café*) Coffee.

Fiambre: Stiff, dead body, corpse.

Fifí: Elegant, neat, smart appearance. Synonym in lunfardo: *pituco*. "You think that by speaking formally, smoking english tobacco strolling through Sarandí and cutting your sideburns like Rodolfo makes you fifí".

Gambetear: To avoid. Synonym in lunfardo: *zafar*. To break free/get out of.

Garpar: (Metathesis of *pagar*) Pay. Give somebody what you owe him/her.

Garrón: An awkward situation / to scrounge something off somebody.

Gil: Fool. Lack of understanding and reasoning. Synonyms in lunfardo: *opa:* chump. "And besides, you run the risk to be nicknamed *gil*".

Gringo: Blond person with white skin; usually refers to foreign people.

Jeta: Face.

Laburo: Work.

Lienzos: Pants. Synonym in lunfardo for *lompas*.

Ligar: To win something / be lucky in games of chance.

Lompas: Pants. Synonym in lunfardo: *lienzos*.

Macana: Craftiness / Stupid thing / Something that went wrong. "Watch out for overwork stop doing *macanas* sleep on a feather mattress and eat with champagne".

Mersa: Tacky, of bad taste, flashy, used generally to describe individuals or circumstances.

Morfar: To eat. "When you tear out your shoes trying to make some money money to *morfar*".

Morfi: Food. "If I earn my *morfi* each day I don't care about the dictionary nor talking with distinction".

Mufa: Bad luck / the person who brings bad luck.

Opa: Fool, Chump / dumb. Synonym in lunfardo: *gil* / excessively slow-witted.

Pebete: Young person / teen. "While a nice *pebeta* pretty like a flower waits under the still light of a lamp".

Perejil: An insignificant person, intrascendent. A peanut. "Because of you, then like a *perejil* I went from fool to fool and then croaked hey, Tango, hey".

Picaflor: Womanizer. Man who flirts with various women at the same time.

Pilchas: Clothes, Apparel. Glad rags. "Youngman frequenter of cafés embellished with poor *pilchas* happy with the fortune that he doesn't have a coin".

Piña: Thump, Punch.

Pinta: Person of good looks / person physically pleasant. Also used to refer to the contrary; of doubtful aspect, not reliable.

Pirar: To go crazy, to go out of one's mind/ get angry.

Pituco: Snob, elegant and well-mannered person. Synonym in lunfardo: *fifí*.

Pollerudo: Henpecked, man that always accepts women's orders, dependent on women, dominated.

Punga: Thief, somebody who steals as soon as he/she has the chance.

Rajar: Escape, run away, to overcome danger. Synonym in lunfardo: *zafar*. To wriggle out

Rata: Austere / stingy, scant in spending.

Roña: Dirtiness.

Sanata: Lies, far-fetched excuses. Synonym in lunfardo: *chamuyo*.

Surtir: To beat. Synonym in lunfardo: fajar.

Timba: Gamble. "No more horse races, the *timba* is over a tough end, never again".

Trampa: Infidelity, being unfaithful to husband or wife.

Trucho: fake, phony / something of poor quality.

Yapa: Extra bit / to throw in a bit extra for free / situation where buyer obtains a gift or extra benefit from the seller.

Yegua: Woman of great seductive charm, voluptuous, femme fatale.

Yiro: whore, street woman.

Zafar: Escape, run away, to overcome danger.

Tango and films

The first Argentine sound movie was released in 1933, at least the first one from a formal viewpoint. Its title was **Tango!** and nearly all the most-celebrated female singers of those days took part in it. For decades, the tango was part of the Argentine film production but that is not the approach here, rather, it is practically the opposite: How foreign films took Argentine tango, and, specifically, how the very tango dance was incorporated.

Does anyone remember Rudolph Valentino in his interpretation of **La cumparsita**? It was a scene in **Los cuatro jinetes del Apocalipsis (Four Horsemen of the Apocalypse)**, a 1923 silent movie. The handsome Italian actor, based on whom Hollywood invented the Latin lover figure, represented a young Argentine bohemian painter. On the scene, accompanied by **La cumparsita**, Valentino, in a gaucho outfit with a whip hanging from the side, passionately tangoes with a woman wrapped in a very Spanish Manila shawl, at a ghastly tavern nestled, at an improbable La Boca neighborhood.

This dance blazed a trail and it suffice to watch Billy Wilder´s **Una Eva y dos Adanes (Some Like it Hot)**, James Cameron´s **Mentiras verdaderas (True Lies)** and Martin Brest´s **Perfume de Mujer (Scent of a Woman)** movies to find this style that ended up being called American tango, though many assume that it is a form of the Argentine tango. In the first movie, Jack Lemmon, dressed as woman, dances **La cumparsita** with Joe Brown. In **True Lies**, Arnold Schwarzenegger, in the role of an absurd spy, interprets **Por una cabeza** by Gardel and Le Pera. Al Pacino tangoes this same song, in the role of a cantankerous retired military, in **Scent of a Woman**. The producers wanted to use **Vida mía** but the heirs of the author, Osvaldo Fresedo, asked for an astronomical amount of money. Therefore, they chose Gardel´s tango, whose intellectual property rights were already in the public domain.

But only the evident eroticism that overflows **Last Tango in Paris** may explain the title of the film, because of the misconception that the words "tango" and "eroticism" are synonyms. There is no tango there: not even in its dance or in its music, nothing, aside from the fact that the main characters meet at a "tango bar" in Paris and that the music was composed by Gato Barbieri, an Argentine composer, although he is a jazz composer.

Arthur Murray, the most celebrated American professor of ballroom dance, described the American tango style in the mid-30s: "In general, basic tango steps are not very different from fox-trot steps. However, such steps, even in the ballroom version, must always have something of the long, gracious and swaying strides of the tough gauchos who originated the tango in the land of *pampas*".

Virulazo

There surely were dancers as good as Virulazo or even better, before and after him. However, maybe more than any other, he represents that strong contrast between physical contexture and skills, origins and history, real personality and stage show of so many popular dancers. Although he was definitely an obese man, he was supremely elegant on stage and was admired, together with his partner Elvira, by celebrities from all over the world in the **Tango Argentino** show. Jorge Martín Orcaizaguirre, Virulazo's real name, was born from a modest family and as a child he used to work as a shoeshine boy and as a peon at a slaughterhouse, among other jobs. He tangoed since he was thirteen and his professional experience was gained in cafés and cabarets of Rosario and Buenos Aires. In 1984 Carlos Segovia and Héctor Orezzolli were looking for dancers for **Tango Argentino** and they found Virulazo and Elvira, who, in those days, made a living only by illegal gambling.

He was an irredeemable porteño, and became cosmopolitan by force. There is an anecdote that one night, at a party to honor Tango Argentino's cast in New York -or was it in Hollywood?- a rather imperative blonde asks Virulazo to take her out to dance. As the dance ends, they break apart, and Virulazo asks Anthony Quinn: "Who is that shorty?". It was Madonna.

38

The carnival

The tango, given its own nature, couldn´t but reflect in its lyrics, the rites and spirit of carnival: The ephemeral joys, the hubbub that hides grief, the mystery of identities behind the masks. Though there is certain flair of fresh innocence on the verses of **Cascabelito** (Little bell) -"Where are you Cascabelito, joyous little mask, so beautiful and playful with your crystal smile-, this is, in no way, the most frequent tone. The same theme acquires a dramatic attitude at **Siga el corso** (by Anselmo Aieta and Fracisco García Jiménez): "Take off the mask! I want to meet you! Your eyes through the *corso* (costumed parade) are looking for my anxiety. Your laughter does me wrong! Show yourself as you are! Behind your miseries carnival is all year round". In **Yo me quiero disfrazar** (I want to disguise), also by Aieta and García Jimenez, the carnival theme is the excuse to talk about the betrayed love, once again: "This new Carnival will not go away without the grimace of my laughter. I want to disguise and dance until the Ash Wednesday. Someone tell that unfaithful woman, that love gambled with two cards, that I was seen disguised, laughing… until I cried!". The verses of **Todo el año es carnaval** (Carnival is all year round) (Julio de Caro, Dante Linyera) display a desperate skepticism: "If love treats you bad, who cares about love? Put on some other disguise to hide your heart… Carnival is all year round, c´mon let´s dance and laugh, 'cause this world is a mess and we have to die one day…".

39

The fallen woman

First, there was the neighborhood, the *conventillo*, the honest working mother, the naïve plaits, the percale dress. Later, the deviation: libertine men, cabaret, champagne, jewelry, fashionable clothes. At the end of the road, poverty again, but now unworthy poverty, loneliness, and the sad hospital bed.

Not every fate is equally unhappy but stories are not that different: **Madame Ivonne**, **Flor de fang**o (Mud flower), **Margot**, **Zorro gris** (Grey old fox), **El motivo** (The reason), **Mano a mano** (We're even), **Ivette**, **Milonguita**, among other tangos, speak of lost women, dragged with lies or by pure vocation, to a dissolute life.

Percale, that low cost cotton material, appears as the symbol of a better past that many of them would like to forget. Margot, the character of the same-name tango, wears silk expensive underwear; however, something about her reveals her origin. That person who is talking to her -may be an old lover- cannot figure out if it is her way of looking, seating or talking which reveal her plebeian origin, most probably, her origin is disclosed by that body that once wore percale clothes. **Milonguita**, the tango that makes reference to the pentant sinner mention said cheap fabric too. The woman who was called Estercita when young, and now is called Milonguita, would give her soul away to change her costly silk clothes for a simple percale dress.

40

Tango fever around the world

The first tango epidemic was long and cruel. Argentine writer Ricardo Güiraldes, rancher, great dancer and habitué of Parisian dance halls, danced one night of 1910 in a party that gathered the most selected celebrities of the French aristocracy and banking. First admired by this circumstantial audience, the dance that came from faraway Buenos Aires succeeded immediately in the most elegant circles of Paris and beyond. Tango dance was introduced in ballrooms, theaters, cafés and big hotels. The "tea-tangos", "conference-tango" and "exhibition-tango" flourished, as well as shows, such as **Le Tango** or **Le Roi du Tango**. The word tango appeared as commercial trade mark of all kinds of products: corsets, dresses, perfumes, champagne, cigarettes and electric bulbs. Sales of a silk, named magic-tango, blending orange, pink and yellow colors, rapidly increased.

At a dance competition organized by the Palais de Glace in Paris, the winning couple danced sixty tangos uninterruptedly.

In England a journalist commented: "From the most aristocratic London hotel to the most humble six-penny tea tango, thousands have been bitten by this tropical tarantula". An Italian reporter wrote from Berlin in 1914: "Two months have passed and there is no other topic of conversation in this city than tango; it is the theme of humorous and satiric comics". Emperor William prohibited his army officials to tango when wearing uniform. In Italy the fever was so extended that the Vatican had to intervene to moderate the most lustful expressions. The tango arrived in

Dancing tango in Florence, Italy

Japan in 1926 brought by the legendary Barón Megata, who after coming from Paris with a collection of records and liking for dance, opened a free academy for the Japanese aristocracy.

The second tango epidemic starts in 1983 and continues until present. The year corresponds to the opening of the musical **Tango Argentino** in Paris with a casting of Argentine dancers and musicians. After the excellent response of the critics the success was booming. In the street, covered with snow, people stood in long queues to get tickets. After November 11, the opening night at the Châtelet theater, the foyer was so crowded that the floor was officially declared in danger of collapse.

143

**Tango in Piazza
Duomo in Catania
Page 144: Dancing
tango in the old city
of Split, Croacia**

At that moment **Tango Argentino** starts to be internationally celebrated: First in Europe, later in the United States, after that, around the world. In 1985, the show is presented in New York, where it is recognized by all imaginable celebrities, from Lady Di to Frank Sinatra, from Rudolf Nureyev to Kirk Douglas. Prestigious critic Clive Barnes wrote in the New York Post: "Run, run, just run as quickly as you can to the City Center, where you can delight your eyes, minds and hearts with **Tango Argentino**". Barnes ends his article with: "As far as I am concerned, I wholeheartedly wish to travel to Buenos Aires as soon as possible and learn to dance tango. Not necessarily in that order". These words were involuntarily prophetic: Little by little, the tango dance started to gain followers not only in Europe, not only in the United States, countries in Africa, Asia, and Oceania were already gripped by this nonstop fever.

41
The tango lesson

The tango dance is not only a string of steps, a style and accompanying music. Dancing tango entails accepting the need to overcome many difficulties and in order to master a fairly basic skill one must learn it one way or other: through formal training, as it is the usual now, or the informal way, as it was done in the past. In other words, the ability transmission process that tango requires is neither simple nor brief. In other times, men learnt through friends, uncles, older brothers or more experienced dancers. Women, on the other hand, learnt everything they needed to know -always at a less complex level than men- through their male relatives, at meetings or family parties.

For the last two decades, in Buenos Aires, as well as in the rest of the world, tango lessons are conducted by professors, instructors, and all kind of teachers. What must one know to dare get out on the dance floor? The man has the greatest responsibility: First, learn to "walk" the tango; second, establish a set of steps, and the talent to improvise the order to dance those steps; third develop the ability to guide the woman and make her understand, without words, which figures and steps he wants her to do; finally, play around with these elements while "drifting" to the music in the midst of

a usually packed dance floor.

An extra difficulty: Each orchestra, whose recordings are played at milongas, has a particular characteristic, rhythm and style; therefore, the way of dancing also differs... or should differ. It is not the same dancing a tango to a recording of Juan D´Arienzo orchestra -with a very marked compass and fast tempo- than dancing music played by Carlos Di Sarli´s orchestra with its slow and melodic tangos. If we understand that the steps repertoire is practically endless, we can deduct that, ideally, the process of learning tango never ends.

As evidenced by the two or three specialized magazines in Buenos Aires, the offer of tango lessons grew and diversified amazingly lately. In addition to the expected courses for beginner, intermediate and advanced learners, or the classes about tango rhythms and milonga, other proposals are advertised as: "Tango milonguero with figures to show off", "Communication and creativity", "Secrets of the step, the axis, and posture", "Seminar on the embrace", as well as an impossible "Learn tango in five classes" and a very curious "Tango Zen".

Cabecear

Among the eighteen meanings that the Dictionary of the Spanish Royal Academy (Real Academia Española, RAE) provide for the word *cabecear* (to head), there is one missing: the delicate head nod that a man makes towards a woman with the discreet purpose of asking her out to dance in a tango dance hall of Buenos Aires, today just like fifty years ago. The woman will reply with an extremely subtle head movement if she accepts the invitation. If not, she will elegantly ignore him.

The head modality has a lot of social wisdom: if the man is rejected, nobody will notice it. It would have been different if the man had crossed through the dance floor and approached the lady in question and she, with despise or with kindness, who would care, had said "go back to your table, I have no intention of dancing with you". How can one recover from such humiliation?

Cabecear is an art and a science: It is convenient to be neither too self-confident nor excessively shy and one has to aim the prey with little error. It is not unusual that two women sitting side by side stand up at the same time to go out to dance because each understood the sign was aimed at her.

Anyone who visits a milonga today may study the numerous shades and effects of the *cabeceo*, and most probably one or more absent-minded men that stand up and walk straight to the woman with which they want to dance. They are usually foreigners or beginners. It is known of many foreigners that devote as much time to get the exact point of the head nod in front of the mirror as to master the most complicated tango steps.

42

Electronic tango

If the so-called electronic tango is more tecno than tango or more tango than tecno it may sound as a tongue twister but it is a serious question. The protagonists of this movement, that some prefer to label *tango fusión* (new tango), born in the 90's with the trendsetting groups Gotan Project and Bajofondo Tango Club, including present groups, decided to maintain certain tango elements but immersed into a sea of electronic processes, sustained by the steady beat, so-called *machacón* (monotonous beat), characteristic of techno music. The sound of digitally processed acoustic ins-

Bajofondo Tango Club

truments and the presentation of video clips give electronic tango a characteristic packaging, relatively common to all groups.

The controversy is still alive and opinions vary from firm defense to straight disapproval: "We wanted to get rid of the tedious and dark side of tango to make it more pop and cheerful", an example of the first opinion as stated by musician Leo Satragno. The *bandoneón* player Rodolfo Mederos, on the other side firmly states "tecnotango is a form of ignorance".

44

People who consider that the stage tango, with its figures even acrobatics, is less authentic than the tango danced on the dance floors, surely do not know about its evolution and the influence that one had on the other. Professional artists have always taken steps from the dance floor and vice versa.

In the 30s the tango show was presented under a format that still persists today: the *revista*, a musical variety show, with a live orchestra and dancers, and a recreation of the different moments of tango history. In the last two decades, such basic model varied very little: An *arrabalero* beginning with two men dancing, and a final act with a tango by Piazzolla. For the closing, **La cumparsita** with the whole company on stage. These very same elements are used by first class shows as much as by acceptable ones or truly mediocre performances. The for export tango show has also big differences. On one hand, those shows plagued with as many clichés as one could imagine, tangos played a thousand times and robotic dancers; on the other, the show performed by knowledgeable people who dares to go beyond what a tourist presumably expects to watch and listen.

However, if one had to mention only one example of a tango show, **Tango Argentino**, so much quoted, cannot be overlooked. The release of this musical variety show in Paris, in November 1983, marked the beginning of an unprecedented phenomenon in popular culture and art. The tango music and even more the tango dance, of the Río de la Plata, which was in danger of extinction, thrived unexpectedly. The directors of **Tango Argentino**, Claudio Segovia and Héctor Orezzolli, created a show that gathered dancers, musicians and singers chosen for being representatives of a noble tradition rather than for their physical aspect or technical conditions. The dance cast was particularly unexpected: The average age was above fifty. Each couple had created its own performance, which produced a variety of distinctive styles and personalities that ended up reflecting the hidden richness of the genre. Claudio Segovia had created the "scruffy-chic" formula to define these artists: "It was the way to explain the great ´class´ of these artists who performed an art of popular origin, ´class´ in the sense

of category, distinction", he explained years later. A critic of the Parisian newspaper Le Figaro wrote after the premiere: "Claudio Segovia and Héctor Orezzolli bring to light the quintessence of a century of night clubs and cabarets of Buenos Aires. Two captivating hours to which the exclusive black color of the costume give a haughty rigor. Tuxedos, suits, dresses, and cloaks, all in black with a slight touch of white and renovated luxury: shiny outfits, whispering skirts, fuseaux and furs in the Poiret fashion… these ladies' wardrobe is full of resources". The first days the show was hired to perform at the Venice Festival and for a tour around France and Italy. The directors also received a first proposal to take **Tango Argentino** to Broadway. The opening night in New York had again a tremendous success. A Newsweek a little bit overstated review said: "Explosive and implosive, tender and tortuous, a combination of pure dance power with erotic energy; nothing can be simpler and nothing can be sexier".

45

Rubato

In Italian, "rubato" means "stolen", in music, it means something very specific: A minimal duration fraction taken from the tempos of the piece. That robbed tempo may be given to another measure or beat or not, but it speeds up or slows down the regular tempo of the score, typical of tango.

The rubato is not indicated in the score, there is no way to do it, and it may only be indicated by the conductor or the soloist. It is for this reason that a non-Argentine musician's orchestra finds it difficult to reproduce the genuine rhythm of a tango. It is useless to look for it in the score and, above all, the way to generate that particular rubato rhythm is not in their history or ear culture.

It is not a tango exclusive condition. The Viennese waltz is executed with rubato too and there is no other orchestra in the world that plays it like a Viennese orchestra.

46

Erotism

A great Argentine scholar had a definite opinion about tango's erotic character. To Carlos Vega this dance was already so complex when born, because of its figures, that the original dancers had a simple dilemma to figure out "we either hold close or we step on each other". And they decided to hold close. "Nothing to do with lust in the embrace", wrote Vega, "the dancers had many other things to worry about".

Even in these days, when customs are much freer, it is practically impossible to find an amateur dancing couple that displays an erotic behavior at the milonga dance floor. Tango requires deep concentration and other type of focus: The man and the woman do not smile or look at each other while they dance, they do not look around.

However, tango dance has reserved a space for erotism. That is the case of stage tango, where passionate figures swirl around, lips come closer, looks melt down, the man's hand caresses the woman's legs, and the embrace tightens to impossible limits. But, this open erotism may, either be reduced to a series of stereotyped gestures -ending up in a caricature-, or be interpreted from the sensuality of the original dance, dramatized for the stage.

47

The mother

Tango mothers are not evil, tyrannical nor spiteful; they are not lazy nor love luxury. The little old woman who is bended over the sink washing others' clothes to make ends meet, represents other many tango mothers, all of them equally selfless and specially loyal to the son who has taken the wrong path and has been the death of her. There are always the sons who sing to these good women, regret their ruin and return as small boys to the maternal lap.

In the so-many-times-interpreted tango **La casita de mis viejos** (My folks' little house), there is a well-off mother, as one can assume from the simple circumstance that it is an old servant, a completely strange figure in tango lyrics, who welcomes the son who returns, tired and defeated, to his parents' house after a long time. However, in this undoubtedly wealthy family, the lady of the house is, to the protagonist, simply his poor old mom. Sick, kindhearted and comprehensive as the humblest mom of a *conventillo* she welcomes her son without complaints or reproof.

The embrace

"To embrace" means to take and hold in the arms as a sign of love and "embrace" is the act of embracing. These are the definitions given in the elemental dictionary, Pequeño Larousse Ilustrado. However, in the tango dance the meaning of "embrace" goes beyond that definition referred to "the act of embracing" and becomes a key element in terms of contemporary floor dancing.

Much has been said and much has been discussed regarding the correct forms, the elegance or about the practice of embracing one person to another when dancing tango.

There is a very-well known classification of embraces depending on the dance style. Milonguero style or *tango del centro* is danced in a very close embrace, chest-to-chest; in *salon tango* the couple embraces but with a slight separation; in the *nuevo tango* the embrace is flexible to make room for figures.

However, this classification is not sufficient: Other variables exist, depending on the height of the arms of the man. Some men's arms are put around a lady's waist, in such case it would be an open embrace; or if the arms are placed on the woman's shoulder -sometimes too close- causing a suffocating effect on the woman; or under the shoulder, a firm arm and loose hand; this is the paradigm of the perfect union.

What about women? The arm's position placed gently around the man's neck, in

a way so that the hand rests over the shoulder blade of her partner. This style, although rarely used, can still be seen.

Another position used by the elder female dancers, also occasionally by the young ladies, consists of holding the partner slightly, with the hand smoothly crossed back on a down-up direction. The position that the arm is crossing in diagonal holding almost the man's entire back is a new trend in the last years and it not easy to know its origins. Some malicious persons have suggested that it is another effect derived from this sort of "new masculinity": the arm placed that way looks as if the woman's arm is protecting her partner and it is quite accepted today that men hold the right to be considered vulnerable.

Somebody ventured an opinion regarding the origins of the embrace in the tango dance: it might derive from the need of affection of those European immigrants that arrived in Buenos Aires at the turn-of-the-century, leaving behind their home and family, and that become the social stratum from which, to a large extent tango culture was born.

A century later, curiously coupled with this concept in the sense of the warmth and intimacy that the term "embrace" provides, it was transformed into an interesting "for export" article as a constituent element of the tango and usually sounds in the ears of foreign amateurs with no fewer suggestions and a no less fascination that the word "pampa".

49

Orchestra conductors

The tango personality changed throughout time without losing its nature and identity. Composers, interpreters, poets, and, in a decisive manner, orchestra conductors have influenced such changes and personality. The conductor here must not be understood as the baton that conducts the symphonic orchestra. In tango, orchestra conductors represent, above all, the creation or recreation of styles: orchestration, rhythmic accentuation, and harmony. In many cases, they have been also the authors of a great number of central pieces of the live repertoire.

Is it possible to come up with a listing of the best orchestras of the history of tango? Tough task: Even the most important ones went through different periods, therefore: What period should one pick up from such and such director? On the other hand, there were perhaps not so extraordinary orchestras from the musical point of view, but which were excellent bands and great companions of the social dance. Finally, personal taste comes in: The enthusiastic admirer of Osvaldo Pugliese may not feel a similar fondness for Fresedo. Anyway, these two musicians would be on a preliminary list of conductors of the highest level. Together with them, and for different reasons Francisco Canaro, Pedro Láurenz, Carlos Di Sarli, Aníbal Troilo, and Julio De Caro.

Page 173: Osvaldo
Pugliese in Teatro
Solís in Montevideo

Francisco Canaro

Precisely De Caro (1899-1980), the great vanguardist of his days, introduced harmonic and melodic innovations that created a truly school, the "decareana" school. Composer of academic instruction and popular sensitivity, he started recording in 1924 with who would be his famous sextet. Among many other contributions, he enabled soloists to stand out, among them, his own brother Francisco, pianist, as well as bandoneón players Pedro Láurenz y Pedro Maffia. It is said that the tango that we listen to today exists because De Caro existed. Many decades later, Astor Piazzolla, paid tribute to De Caro with his piece **Decarísimo**, an acknowledgement that many tango musicians, and Piazzolla himself, owed him.

As far as orchestras specially devoted to perform dancing music -not because the above orchestras did not do so, very much to the contrary- the top historic name is Juan D'Arienzo. This violinist and composer imposed a change in the rhythmic marking, inspired by the great American jazz bands, with which he attracted to dance clubs thousands of enthusiasts. Other beautiful orchestras, very much loved by dancers, were and still are Ricardo Tanturi, Miguel Caló, Lucio Demare, Alfredo De Angelis, Angel D'Agostino's orchestras, all of them associated to really distinctive voices. It is not necessary to listen to tango for a long time to be able to identify the sound of the major orchestras. The sound of a Troilo, a Pugliese, a Di Sarli, a Fresedo is so characteristic and unforgettable at the same time. It is worth mentioning three more names of extensive history, who are practically active nowadays: Mariano Mores (1922), author of celebrated pieces such as **Gricel**, **Cuartito azul** (Little blue room), **Cafetín de Buenos Aires** (Little café in Buenos Aires), **Adiós Pampa mía** (Good bye my pampa), broadened the format of the typical orchestra and took it to a symphonic scale. Horacio Salgán (1916), virtuous and original pianist, went from his typical orchestra in 1947 to his famous duo with Ubaldo De Lío. Finally, Leopoldo Federico (1927), extraordinary bandoneón player and innovative musician, had also diverse groups and continues to take tango around the world.

Leopoldo Federico

Mariano Mores

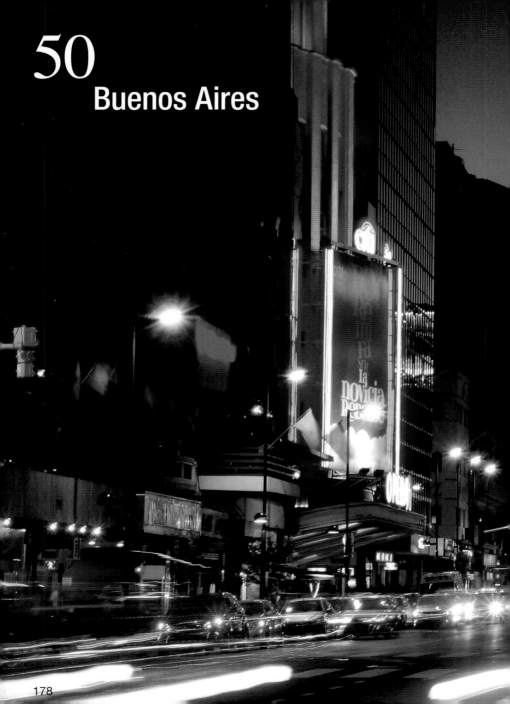

50
Buenos Aires

Buenos Aires, Queen of Plata
Buenos Aires, my beloved land
Here is my song
And my life with it goes.

The word porteño identifies those people born in port cities of Spain, Venezuela, Colombia and Argentina. Therefore, those of us who were born in Buenos Aires are porteños because during long, very long decades the city had a port. This relationship is not enough, however, without a key piece of information: being a porteño means having been born in Buenos Aires and grown up listening to tangos, regardless if it was an election or a fatality, a taste or an accident. The circle is closed with the evidence that in the history of this genre that we use to call *rioplatense* (due to its relation to the Río de la Plata) the existence of the port played a crucial role.

Most probably brought by sailors through the port of Buenos Aires, *la habanera*, a Cuban dance of European origin contributed significantly to the configuration of the primitive tango. Likewise, through the port of Buenos Aires, hundreds of thou-

sands of Italian, Spanish, Jewish from Central Europe, Syrians and Lebanese immigrants arrived in Buenos Aires. A great number of them settled in the city yearning for home and condemned to melancholy and loneliness; these feelings fed what would be later the characteristic music of this mixed city.

We could imagine Buenos Aires as the construction, throughout time, of a big stage, or even better, multiple stages for tango. These were the first *arrabales* (suburbs) and *conventillos*: La Boca, Corrales Viejos -nowadays Parque de los Patricios-, Miserere -today Once neighborhood-, Bajo Belgrano, Palermo. Alongside, the brothel areas, where men used to practice tango steps between themselves while waiting for their turn. It is believed that it was at the academies of what today is Tribunales (in the past this neighborhood was called Parque) that tango was played for the first time within the perimeter of the city, and danced for the first time at a so-called "Almacén de Machado", in the intersection of Solís and Estados Unidos streets, surely a false statement since the tango dance is a fruit that ripens slowly.

However, it is known that wealthy boys went to the famous Hansen restaurant at the Palermo woods, among others, as well as to "Lo de Laura", a ghastly spot at the intersection of Paraguay and Ecuador. Tango was listened to in the street. It was played by the barrel organs and its sound slipped through the window blinds of middle-class neighborhood houses. Young ladies used to practice at the piano the scores of **El choclo** and **La morocha**, passed from hand to hand when the tango still had a bad reputation. Not many years later, the high class danced it at the Colón Theater on the space used for carnival celebrations.

Despite the changes, fashions, ebbs and flows, Buenos Aires still is, even imperceptibly, a tango city, though, sometimes in a rather forced manner and others in a quite fictitious way. However, every time a taxi driver navigates through the city listening to a radio tango show and knows the tango name, orchestra and singer, one can confirm that the sap is still circulating and the tree is alive.

Aditional information

Bibliography

Alonso, Alberto: *Así nació La Cumparsita*. Ed. Mosca. Montevideo, 1967.

Alposta, Luis: *El tango en Japón*. Ed.Corregidor. Buenos Aires, 1987.

Amuchástegui, Irene y Del Priore, Oscar: *Cien tangos fundamentales*. Ed. Alfaguara/Aguilar. Buenos Aires, 2008.

Autores varios (with the compilation of Ramón Pelinski): *El tango nómada*. Ed. Corregidor. Buenos Aires, 2000.

Benedetti, Héctor Ángel: *Las mejores letras de tango. Antología de 250 letras, cada una con su historia*. Ed. Seix Barral. Buenos Aires, 1998.

Collier, Simon: *Carlos Gardel, su vida, su música, su época*. Ed. Sudamericana. Buenos Aires, 1999.

De Lara, Tomás y De Panti, Inés: *El tema del tango en la literatura argentina (antología)*. Ed. Culturales Argentinas. Buenos Aires, 1968.

Del Mazo, Mariano y D'Amore, Adrián: *Juan Carlos Copes, una vida de tango*. Ed. Corregidor. Buenos Aires, 2001.

Del Priore, Oscar: *Osvaldo Pugliese, una vida en el tango*. Ed. Losada. Buenos Aires, 2008.

Ferrer, Horacio: *El libro del tango*. Antonio Tersol Editor. Buenos Aires. 1980.

Gobello, José y Amuchástegui, Irene: *Vocabulario ideológico del lunfardo*. Ed. Corregidor. Buenos Aires, 1998.

Lamas, Hugo y Binda, Enrique: *El tango en la sociedad porteña (1880-1920)*. Ed. Hector Lucci. Buenos Aires, 1998.

Martini Real, Juan Carlos (responsable de la edición): *Historia del tango (antología)*. Ed. Corregidor. Buenos Aires, 1976.

Matamoro, Blas: *La ciudad del tango*. Ed. Galerna. Buenos Aires, 1969.

Pujol, Sergio: *Historia del baile (de la milonga a la disco)*. Ed. Emecé. Buenos Aires, 1999.

Pujol, Sergio: *Discépolo. Una biografía argentina*. Ed. Emecé. Buenos Aires, 1997.

Rossi, Vicente: *Cosas de negros*. Ed. Hachette. Buenos Aires, 1958.

Salas, Horacio: *El tango, una guía definitiva*. Editorial Aguilar. Buenos Aires, 1996.

Tallon, José Sebastián: *El tango en sus etapas de música prohibida*. Cuadernos del Instituto Amigos del Libro Argentino. Buenos Aires, 1959.

Vega, Carlos (with the edition of Coriún Aharonián): *Los orígenes del tango argentino*. Editorial de la Universidad Católica Argentina. Buenos Aires, 2007.

Zucchi, Oscar *El tango, el bandoneón y sus intérpretes*. Editorial Corregidor, 1998.

Discography

Carlos Gardel: Discografía completa (fifty CDs). Ediciones Altaza.

El inolvidable Julio De Caro y su sexteto típico (1926-1928). El Bandoneón.

Julio De Caro (1929-1932). Disco Pampa-EMI.

Libertad Lamarque. Lantower, Grandes del Tango.

Mercedes Simone: antiguos temas de colección. EMI-DBN.

Rosita Quiroga: apología tanguera. El Bandoneón.

Nelly Omar: desde entonces. Euro Records-EMI, Archivo Odeón.

Tita Merello. Lantower, Grandes del tango.

Ada Falcón con el acompañamiento de la orquesta de Francisco Canaro: sus mayores éxitos. EMI-DBN.

Azucena Maizani: La Ñata Gaucha. El Bandoneón.

Las grandes orquestas del tango: Juan D'Arienzo. 40 grandes éxitos. Maestros del Tango Argentino.

Juan D'Arienzo y su orquesta típica. Canta Héctor Mauré: sus primeros éxitos. BMG-RCA.

Angel D'Agostino-Angel Vargas: tango de los ángeles. BMG-RCA.

Carlos Di Sarli y su orquesta típica. Instrumental. BMG-RCA.

Carlos Di Sarli. Canta Roberto Rufino: sus primeros éxitos. BMG-RCA.

Carlos Di Sarli y su orquesta típica. Canta Alberto Podestá: sus primeros éxitos. BMG-RCA.

Lucio Demare y su orquesta: sus primeros éxitos. EMI-DBN. Colección Reliquias.

Lucio Demare y su orquesta: sus éxitos con Raúl Berón. EMI-DBN

Edmundo Rivero (1950-1953). Euro Records.

Edmundo Rivero: esencia criolla. Universal Music.

Osvaldo Pugliese y su orquesta típica. Polygram.

Osvaldo Pugliese: instrumentales inolvidables. EMI-DBN.

Osvaldo Pugliese: sus éxitos con Alberto Morán. EMI-DBN

Miguel Caló: al compás del corazón (singer Raúl Berón). EMI-DBN.

Ricardo Tanturi y su orquesta típica Los Indios (cantan Alberto Castillo, Enrique "Aníbal Troilo Pichuco y su orquesta típica (instrumental) 1941-1944". BMG-RCA.

Aníbal Troilo Pichuco y su orquesta típica. Canta Floreal Ruiz. Amor y tango. BMG-RCA.

Aníbal Troilo Pichuco y su orquesta típica. Canta Fiorentino. Yo soy el tango. BMG-RCA.

Aníbal Troilo Pichuco y su orquesta típica. Canta: Edmundo Rivero. Cafetín de Buenos Aires. BMG-RCA.

Aníbal Troilo Pichuco y Roberto Goyeneche: El Gordo y el Polaco. BMG-RCA.

Aníbal Troilo-Roberto Grela (Cuarteto típico) RCA.

Campos, Osvaldo Ribó y Roberto Videla). Lantower, Grandes del tango.

Astor Piazzolla y su orchestra típica (1946-1948). Frémeaux &Asocies.

Piazzolla… ¿o no? Bailable y apiazolado. Sony-BMG-RCA.

Astor Piazzolla, edición crítica: Antología. Sony-BMG.

Tango puro: Leopoldo Federico y su orquesta. Sony-BMG.

Institution of interest
NATIONAL ACADEMY OF TANGO

De Mayo Ave. 833, 4345-6967,
www.anacdeltango.org.ar

In 1990 the world's first National Academy of Tango was established in Argentina; created and firstly presided by poet Horacio Ferrer. This Academy aims at preserving the artistic heritage that has been granted through tango, and that still persists today. This institution hosts uncountable activities such as seminars, workshops and exhibitions. The Academy also includes the World Tango Museum and the School of Tango (Museo Mundial de Tango y Liceo Superior de Tango).

GOLDEN
UNIVERSE